"Anne Bodmer Lutz, a master educator in solution-focused therapy, provides a clear and engaging guide for those living with depression and anxiety, as well as their clinicians. Having an evidence-based workbook that approaches concerns with a strengths-based lens is a crucial and powerful skill set in today's 'fix it' culture."

—**Mary Ahn, MD**, professor of psychiatry and pediatrics and vice provost for faculty affairs at UMass Chan Medical School, and ICF-credentialed leadership coach

"In this thoughtfully designed workbook, Anne Bodmer Lutz provides clear, actionable strategies for creating an empowering mindset. Strongly grounded in research, *The Solution-Focused Mindset for Anxiety and Depression* includes nuanced insights about the power of words, empathy, and neuroscience. It offers simple steps that will benefit anyone struggling with depression or anxiety."

—**Alex Korb, PhD**, author of *The Upward Spiral*

"Anne Bodmer Lutz delivers a unique and valuable book that teaches how to use solution-focused brief therapy techniques to manage anxiety and depression in a clear and practical way. *The Solution-Focused Mindset for Anxiety and Depression* is a one-of-a-kind workbook that contain many useful exercises, and is an important resource for mental health wellness."

—**Johnny S. Kim, PhD, LCSW**, professor at the University of Denver Graduate School of Social Work, and author of *Solution-Focused Brief Therapy*

"This book is a great resource for anyone wanting to learn concrete skills for becoming friends with your emotions, reducing suffering, tapping into your inner strength, and cultivating hope (agency with a plan) to improve the quality of your life."

—**Nathalie Edmond, PsyD**, director of counseling at Villanova University, and author of *Mindful Race Talk*

"Having had the privilege of experiencing Anne Bodmer Lutz as a solution-focused trainer and speaker, I enthusiastically read *The Solution-Focused Mindset for Anxiety and Depression*. What a wonderful guide this is to harness the power of language to improve your life and better manage your symptoms of anxiety and depression! This robust workbook is full of valuable psychoeducation and user-friendly worksheets that would be a helpful tool for individuals seeking a self-help workbook, and/or to use as a therapy extender."

—**Lori Lamont, MA, LPC, ATR-BC**, professional counselor/art therapist, clinical supervisor, and executive director of outpatient services at Lenape Valley Foundation

"Anne Bodmer Lutz has managed to transmit her wealth of knowledge and experience with solution-focused brief therapy into a wonderful workbook, easily accessible and tremendously helpful. The rich case examples are diverse and relatable. This 'how to' manual of hope for those suffering from anxiety and depression will also be the perfect handbook for therapists, loaded with practical tools and sound advice. It is an inspiring and essential resource for us all."

—**Bobbi Beale, PsyD**, director of the Center for Innovative Practices at Case Western Reserve University, and coauthor of *Adventure Group Psychotherapy*

The Solution-Focused Mindset for Anxiety and Depression

A Workbook to Manage Emotions, Harness Your Strengths, and Feel Better Now

Anne Bodmer Lutz, MD

New Harbinger Publications, Inc.

Publisher's Note

This publication is designed to provide accurate and authoritative information in regard to the subject matter covered. It is sold with the understanding that the publisher is not engaged in rendering psychological, financial, legal, or other professional services. If expert assistance or counseling is needed, the services of a competent professional should be sought.

NEW HARBINGER PUBLICATIONS is a registered trademark of New Harbinger Publications, Inc.

New Harbinger Publications is an employee-owned company.

New Harbinger Publications, Inc.
5720 Shattuck Avenue
Oakland, CA 94609
www.newharbinger.com

Cover design and illustration by Sara Christian

Acquired by Wendy Millstine and Jed Bickman

Edited by Joyce Wu

Library of Congress Cataloging-in-Publication Data on file

Printed in the United States of America

27 26 25

10 9 8 7 6 5 4 3 2 1 First Printing

To John, my amygdala whisperer and steadfast partner in our life's journey.
Thank you for being by my side.

Contents

Foreword

The Solution-Focused Mindset for Anxiety and Depression: A Workbook to Manage Emotions, Harness Your Strengths, and Feel Better Now introduces readers to the proven principles for change from the Solution-Focused Brief Therapy (SFBT). SFBT is an evidence-based mental health intervention that is used worldwide to treat depression, anxiety, and other psychosocial conditions related to interpersonal and behavioral health challenges. As a proven brief therapy, SFBT achieves symptom relief from depression in just four to six sessions for most people and can be effective even in a one session interview (Vermeulen-Oskam et al. 2024; Zak and Pekala 2024). Dr. Anne Bodmer Lutz, a renowned psychiatrist and solution-focused expert, has skillfully translated this effective psychotherapy into a self-help workbook so that you can take advantage of these life-changing principles.

This book will artfully take you through the principles of change from SFBT and provide you with skills and practice exercises to help you achieve your desired outcomes. Reading each chapter is more than accumulating new information; instead, it launches you into a set of thought-provoking questions and reflections that are focused on helping you change your life. The life stories in the chapters show you how the solution-focused change skills have been enacted in the lives of other people. Each chapter unveils a new way of thinking and a set of concrete skills and actions that you can use to improve your depression and anxiety and transform your life.

From the beginning of this book, you learn how to ask yourself skillful questions that require a lot of reflection, including how to examine your goals and progress, using numbers known as scaling questions. Scaling questions are just one example of the important skills that are used in SFBT and that are covered in detail throughout this book. Chapters further provide a plethora of change principles and skills such as how to alter language, how to harness strengths in yourself and within your important relationships, and how to create a preferred future.

Chapter 1 lays the foundation for beginning your journey toward a desired future. This chapter teaches you the pathways of hope, helping you discover the meaning and the power of self-agency for change combined with the strength of a plan that can be enacted through small steps. Chapter 1 sets the stage for later chapters that facilitate change. Chapter 1 further discusses the major tenets of SFBT and the importance of nurturing the solution-focused mindset that will open up possibilities for the changes you desire. Chapters 2 through 7 illustrate major skills from SFBT that professionally trained psychotherapists use to help their clients overcome and cope with depression and anxiety.

Chapter 2 illustrates the power of language to shape meaning and behavior and teaches you how to alter your language to get the changes you desire. You will learn how to crack open the world of words and their meaning and how to use language with positive assumptions. Chapter 3 walks you through how to deal with intense emotions that may be taking over your mind. Intense fear and anger or flight responses are explained to be like having a storm in the brain that needs to be calmed. In this chapter, Dr. Lutz educates you about the architecture of your brain and shows proven, solution-focused techniques that she calls "amygdala whispering." These effective techniques help you calm the storm and move toward thinking more clearly. Chapter 4 discusses the value of important relationships, your social support systems, and significant others. From connecting to people, to pets, and to spiritual resources, our social context matters. There is a clear relationship between depression and loneliness and this chapter shows you how to both cultivate and change relationships to make yourself feel better.

In chapter 5, you discover the power of envisioning your future. In SFBT, asking what are your best hopes helps you discover your goals, aspirations, and what you want your life to be like. This chapter drills down into the details of what it means to develop a preferred future, offering several things you can do to manage your emotions, get past roadblocks in your thinking, and make confident decisions. You will leave chapter 5 with a better understanding about the details of your preferred future. In chapter 6, you revisit again the scaling questions, learning how to use scaling to evaluate your progress toward your preferred future and to take meaningful steps forward. Finally, chapter 7 wraps all the SFBT change principles and skills you have learned in this book up by introducing a solution-focused, four quadrant framework that helps you put all the solution-focused skills together so that you can keep practicing this life-changing approach.

The seven chapters of this book are packed full of life-changing principles from SFBT and is a must read for anyone suffering from depression or anxiety. The skills taught from SFBT are proven psychotherapeutic practices, and Dr. Lutz crafts the skills together into this user-friendly self-help workbook that will challenge your thinking about how to change and will impact your life.

—Cynthia Franklin, PhD, LCSW-S, LMFT
Stiernberg/Spencer Family Professor in Mental Health
Steve Hicks School of Social Work, University of Texas at Austin
Courtesy Professor of Psychiatry and Behavioral Sciences
Dell Medical School, University of Texas at Austin

CHAPTER 1

An Introduction to the Solution-Focused Mindset

Beginning journeys can often feel lonely and daunting as you venture into unexplored territories without a clear direction or a sense of how you'll move forward. Some beginnings launch with great clarity, where you know what you need and the direction to take. Other beginnings are unexpected. They ask for courage, self-compassion, and the patience to navigate your next steps before a new path fully unfolds. Beginnings may catch you off guard, and a new landscape of possibilities is set in motion before you even realize it. In these beginnings, you may be surprised to discover courage and strength to carry on. Unexpected delights and joy might emerge, as well as hope to sustain you. When you remain open to new and rediscovered parts of your life, the full beauty and diversity of who you are will shine through.

When anxiety and depression weigh heavily on you, it's easy to get drawn into a cycle of problems that leaves you feeling overwhelmed and disconnected from life's simple pleasures, like enjoying a peaceful walk, sharing laughter with a friend, or savoring a quiet moment with a loved one. In a fast-paced world, where just getting through the day can feel like a struggle, it's understandable that staying open to new beginnings may seem daunting. The constant stream of news and social media's relentless influence only amplify this disconnection, pulling you further from the present moment.

Yet, in the face of these challenges, despite the heavy burdens you carry, your strength continues to emerge, even when exhaustion tries to take hold. You still manage to care for your family, handling responsibilities with quiet determination, forging ahead one day at a time. Perhaps there's comfort in the shared silence with a loved one, or in the simple joy of sunlight warming your skin, reminding you that even small moments matter. Each day, whether you're preparing a meal or offering a word of encouragement, your resilience shines through. Resilience is about the strength you show as you keep moving forward, showing up with determination time after time, and embracing the quiet power that shines within you.

Solution-focused brief therapy (SFBT) is a compassionate and evidence-based approach that empowers you to weave hope into your daily life, one step at a time (Kim et al. 2019). This approach encourages you to connect with your inner strengths, helping you realize the power within you. It guides you toward creating a plan, no matter how short-term—even if it's just for the next ten minutes. By focusing on those small steps, you begin to harness your resilience and take meaningful action, one moment at a time.

This book is designed to help you cultivate a solution-focused mindset that empowers you to surmount anxiety and depression. By guiding you to recognize and rediscover your strengths, it offers practical tools to help you harness those strengths in the present moment. With a clear plan and actionable steps, you'll find relief as you navigate your challenges and reignite your sense of possibility for the future.

The SFBT approach is a beacon of hope. Born out of the Brief Family Therapy Center in Milwaukee, Wisconsin, visionaries Steve de Shazer and Insoo Kim Berg, together with their team, meticulously observed countless therapy sessions, noting which words and behaviors propelled people toward their goals; anything that didn't contribute to progress was discarded. Through their extensive research, they isolated two key components to a cultivating a solution-focused mindset: repeating what works and having the courage to shift when things aren't going as planned. This is the essence of SFBT. Rooted in positive psychology, this approach highlights success and how to expand on it, rather than dwelling on what's wrong and how to fix it.

The solution-focused approach is the "how-to" of hope, offering practical tools to shift your focus from problems to possibilities. It empowers you to tap into your strengths, take meaningful steps toward change, and create realistic, achievable plans. By reframing challenges and guiding you to focus on what can be achieved, SFBT turns obstacles into opportunities for growth. With its forward-thinking approach, it helps you see new possibilities and take action, actively building hope in your daily life, one step at a time.

Hope is far more than a passing emotion; it acts as a vital force that sustains your mental well-being. It has the power to ignite positive emotions, bringing a sense of fulfillment and joy into your life. Hope doesn't stop there—it strengthens your life satisfaction, fuels your sense of purpose, and enhances the overall quality of your experiences (Long and Gallagher 2018). As Synder, Irving, and Anderson (1991) suggest, hope is anchored in two key elements that shape our ability to persevere and thrive:

- Agency—the belief that you can navigate your path and achieve your goals
- Pathways—the ability to create a plan and identify the steps to move from where you are now to where you want to be

This understanding of hope goes beyond wishful thinking—it's about believing in a clear path forward and trusting in your ability to walk it. How do you cultivate hope? The solution-focused approach transforms it into a personal and empowering journey, one that's unique to you.

How to Use the Exercises in This Book

The exercises in this book support your journey in a way that aligns with your unique needs and preferences. Here are some ways you might choose to approach them:

- **Set your own pace:** Move through the exercises at a comfortable pace, focusing on each question or reflection that comes up and spending extra time on those that resonate deeply with you.
- **Personalize your experience:** Adapt the exercises to fit your situation. If a question doesn't match your current focus, tweak it to align with what matters most. This book supports your unique journey, so adjust the exercises as needed.
- **Reflect or discuss:** Some of you prefer to work through the exercises privately, jotting down thoughts in a journal. Others value discussing them with a trusted friend, partner, or group, allowing for shared insights and perspectives.
- **Mix and match:** You have the freedom to explore the exercises in whichever order feels right for you. As you move through them, you may find yourself naturally drawn to skip ahead to a section that resonates or return to an earlier one with a fresh perspective. Each exercise gently guides you toward what feels most relevant in the moment, shaping your journey in a way that suits your unique path.
- **Take small steps:** When an exercise feels too challenging, consider breaking it down into smaller, more manageable parts. Focus on just one aspect at a time and allow yourself to move forward at a pace that feels right.
- **Reflect on your progress:** As you complete the exercises, consider what you've discovered. Notice which practices bring you the most clarity or comfort, and revisit them as needed.

Whether you're moving from feeling burdened by stress to feeling prepared for life's unpredictable challenges, or from uncertainty to clarity, these exercises will support your growth. How you choose to engage with them is entirely up to you. What matters most is that they provide you with meaningful support and help you gain confidence in navigating your path. But before we delve into exercises, let's take a closer look at emotions and how our bodies respond to them.

As you develop a solution-focused mindset, you'll discover an empowering tool: solution-focused scaling questions—think of a doctor asking you to rate your pain level. However, instead of focusing on the severity of challenges, like rating how anxious or depressed you feel, these scales measure your actions, strengths, and progress. Solution-focused scaling shifts your attention to the confidence, satisfaction, and progress that lead you toward your goals.

As I tell my clients, "There is magic in numbers" (Berg and de Shazer 1993). Scaling questions capture this magic by guiding you from the stress-filled "basement" of your brain to the "upstairs," where rational thinking and clear decision-making take hold.

Your number is uniquely yours, reflecting your personal perspective and choices. In this way, scaling helps you design a clear path forward by highlighting the strategies and actions that have already worked well for you—especially when you ask yourself what keeps your number from being lower and what a "good enough" number is. Understanding what's already working for you and pinpointing the actions and strengths that help you maintain your current level allow you to build upon these strengths and move closer to your desired outcomes. This process ensures that your plan is tailored to your own experiences and successes.

While chapters 1 through 5 introduce some basic scaling questions, chapter 6 will discuss scaling in detail and give you opportunities to practice what I call "working the scale." After you read chapter 6, you may wish to return to exercises throughout this book and work the scale to get even more out of this journey.

Throughout this book, you'll also be encouraged to keep five simple yet powerful questions in mind—*What else? How else? Who else? When else? Where else?* These are more than just prompts; they're tools for expanding your sense of possibility. While not explicitly stated in every exercise, they are key to deepening your reflections and uncovering new perspectives.

Each question serves a purpose: *What else?* encourages deeper reflection on your successes. *How else?* prompts you to explore alternative methods. *Who else?* reminds you of the people who have supported you. *When else?* and *Where else?* push you to consider when and where your strengths have emerged. These questions reveal untapped potential, often hidden in the corners of your mind, opening the door to multiple paths forward and allowing you to explore possibilities you may not have considered before.

The exercises ahead will guide you from the basement of survival-based thinking to the upstairs, where critical thinking opens the door to infinite possibilities. As you shift your focus, you'll reframe your mindset and discover fresh approaches to challenges empowering you to take meaningful action. With each step, you'll build momentum, steadily progressing toward the changes you seek.

For even more exercises, printouts, and downloadable resources, please visit the website for this book at http://www.newharbinger.com/54742. In fact, I'd recommend pausing here to do the online exercise for chapter 1, "Scaling Wellness: Reflective Exercises for Self-Care."

Embracing Your Emotions: Navigating Anxiety and Depression

Your emotions span a wide range—from the comforting to the uncomfortable—and each carries a message. These signals, like an internal compass, guide you toward what you need and what might serve you best as you move through life. They help you assess, adapt, and forge a path forward. Anxiety, for example, is a natural and necessary emotion. When you're faced with danger, it prepares your body, urging you to pause and consider your next steps. But when anxiety overstays its welcome, it can bring unnecessary distress that affects both your mind and your body. Emotions like sadness, grief, and loss also shape your human experience. These feelings arise during difficult times—losing someone close, managing chronic illness, or facing setbacks. In their quiet way, they ask you to slow down, reflect, and discover new ways to navigate life's changes.

While these emotions are natural, they can become more difficult to manage when your responses become rigid. This can make it harder to navigate daily life, pursue your goals, or find joy in the things you once loved. You may catch yourself dwelling on past setbacks, harshly criticizing yourself, or withdrawing from activities and situations that trigger these feelings. Sadness, left unchecked, can evolve into depression, leading to a sense of hopelessness. The things that once brought you pleasure may no longer spark interest. You may also notice changes in your appetite, sleep patterns, or even experience thoughts of self-harm.

Even when emotions feel like they're weighing you down, there's a way to shift your focus—and in doing so, regain the momentum you need to move forward. Resilience is the ability to keep going despite the weight of anxiety and depression. It's when, after a long day of feeling emotionally drained, you get out of bed and take a short walk, knowing that movement, however small, can help lift your mood. It's the moment when, even though your thoughts are racing with self-doubt, you reach out to a friend, seeking support instead of shutting down. Resilience shows up when you wake up feeling hopeless, but still choose to engage in an activity you once enjoyed, trusting that joy will return with time. It's not about eliminating anxiety or depression, but about how you find small ways to cope and rebuild your strength, one step at a time, even on your hardest days.

Resilience is like a snowball rolling down a mountain—it grows depending on where you direct your focus. When you concentrate on your achievements, like setting a healthy boundary, completing a task that felt overwhelming, or finding time for self-care, each success builds momentum, making future challenges easier to manage. But if your attention lingers on setbacks, that snowball can grow heavier with frustration and doubt, making the path ahead feel steeper and holding you back.

The questions you ask yourself are key in shaping this process. By focusing on solution-oriented questions, you shift your mindset toward progress, reminding yourself of the positive actions you've already taken. Each question helps you build a snowball of success, one that propels you forward on the path you truly desire.

Understanding Your Response to Stress and Anxiety

Your response to stress and anxiety is a natural part of how your body operates, deeply connected to your autonomic nervous system. This system has two key parts: the sympathetic and parasympathetic nervous systems. Imagine you sense danger—your sympathetic system steps in like an accelerator, revving up your body to respond. When the danger passes, your parasympathetic system takes over, slowing everything down and bringing you back to a state of calm.

When stress becomes overwhelming, however, your sympathetic system can get stuck in high gear. This often shows up as physical signs like feeling drained, having tense muscles, or experiencing an upset stomach.

To better understand this, think of your brain as having two levels: the "upstairs" and the "basement." Your upstairs, also known as the prefrontal cortex, is the part of your brain that helps you stay organized and focused. It's where critical thinking occurs—where you ask thoughtful questions, evaluate options, and make well-reasoned decisions. Whether you're planning a big project, reflecting on how to approach a difficult conversation, or making choices about self-care, your upstairs brain helps you weigh possibilities and choose a thoughtful path forward.

Solution-focused questions play a key role in helping you stay upstairs. By asking yourself constructive questions like *How have I managed situations like this before? What one small step can I take to improve this situation?* or *How can I use what worked before to help me now?* you engage your upstairs brain. These questions keep you grounded in thoughtful decision-making, allowing you to stay calm and focused, even in difficult situations.

But when stress strikes, your brain often retreats to the basement, where the amygdala and hippocampus take over—activating your survival instincts like fight, flight, or freeze. When this happens, it can feel like you're caught in a storm. Intense emotions start to swirl, and suddenly, what seemed manageable becomes overwhelming. This "storm" clouds your thinking, making it difficult to focus or approach even small tasks.

Recognizing this response can help you find compassion for yourself. When you feel overwhelmed by stress, it's not a personal failure—it's your body reacting to protect you. And just like a storm, it will pass. By giving yourself time and space, you can help calm your nervous system and return to a place of balance, where you can once again use your upstairs brain to navigate through challenges with greater clarity.

To calm this inner storm, you'll learn to use solution-focused techniques that both soothe emotional turbulence and guide you toward calm. These methods will help you access the prefrontal cortex, where you can think clearly, gain insight, and explore options beyond fight, flight, or freeze. Through these practices, you'll begin to treat your emotions with kindness, empathy, and compassion.

Harnessing a Growth Mindset

The solution-focused approach invites you to look beyond the surface of your struggles—shifting your focus from probing deeply to expose the root cause to recognizing the quiet strength that has carried you through. It asks you to uncover the resilience that has been there all along, turning your attention toward the ways you've endured, the obstacles you've overcome, the solutions you've discovered, and a path forward.

Instead of getting caught in what's gone wrong, you tap into your ability to adapt and persevere. With each reflection, you'll begin to realize that your strength isn't only in finding solutions but in the journey itself—showing time and again your remarkable ability to adapt, persevere, and thrive in the face of life's obstacles.

Finding Strengths in Life's Challenges

For many people, revisiting painful events can feel overwhelming and may even make things more difficult. The solution-focused approach offers a different way of engaging with the hardships you face—one that honors your emotions without forcing direct confrontation. It encourages you to focus on how you've successfully handled difficult situations before and helps you discover practical steps for moving forward. By reflecting on your experiences, you'll find positive solutions that empower you to take action while maintaining your emotional well-being.

Take a moment to pause and gently reflect on a difficult experience you've faced, acknowledging how challenging that moment was for you. You don't need to dwell on the details—instead, consider these questions, which are here to help you recognize what supported you through that time and guide you in finding strategies to carry with you as you move forward.

As you answer each question, ask yourself, *What else? Who else?* and *How else?* These prompts will help you go beyond the surface and uncover new possibilities, gently guiding you to recognize the different ways you've already navigated the challenge.

How did you cope with this challenging situation?

____

____

____

____

What was most helpful for you in moving forward?

____

____

____

____

Who noticed your efforts?

____

What would they most appreciate about how you dealt with this challenge?

____

____

What did you learn from this experience?

____

____

____

____

____

On a scale from 1–10, where 10 means you're satisfied with how you coped and 1 is the opposite, how would you rate yourself?

____

How would those most important to you rate your coping skills on the same scale?

____

What would be a good enough number for you to feel satisfied with your efforts? _____

What keeps your rating from being lower?

____

____

What new perspectives did you gain from this experience?

____

____

____

How could this experience benefit you and others?

____

____

____

As you reflect on this exercise, ask yourself whether it was helpful for you, and if so, how was it helpful? What did you discover that would help you navigate future challenges you may face? Consider what new perspectives and possibilities emerged for you—how could you carry these lessons with you in your daily life, shaping your mindset in the moments that matter most?

Nurturing a Solution-Focused Mindset

Tenets are the core principles that shape your thoughts and actions—they are the foundation of how you approach life. When you embrace solution-focused tenets, you foster a mindset that looks for solutions rather than dwelling on problems (Franklin 2012). These ideas help shift your perspective, offering a clearer approach to challenges and unlocking your potential for meaningful change. Think of these tenets as a road map—one that guides you toward a mindset capable of navigating life's complexities with confidence.

Tenets for a Solution-Focused Mindset

If it isn't broken, don't fix it. When you've already solved a problem, there's no need to revisit it with theories or models. The essence of a solution-focused approach is simple: if something works, keep doing it; if it doesn't, try something different. Recognize and build on what's already going well in your life. Your existing strengths can often be your best resource.

No problem happens all the time. Problems aren't constant—they don't happen every moment or in every situation. The fact that you notice a problem means there are also times when things are better. Reflecting on these moments when the problem wasn't present or was more tolerable can provide valuable insights. Understanding these patterns can help you navigate them more effectively.

Small steps can lead to big changes. Progress often begins with small and manageable steps, gradually building over time. Every positive change, no matter how modest, can create a ripple effect that leads to further improvements in your daily life. By focusing on these small shifts, you find yourself moving steadily toward your goals.

If it works, do more of it. When something is working, keep doing it. The key to a solution-focused mindset is to continue with what's already working. Instead of judging the quality of your solutions, focus on their effectiveness. If something has helped before, consider doing it again.

If it's not working, do something different. Repeating familiar patterns is natural, even when they aren't working. But to solve a problem, you need to do something different. A solution-focused mindset is about exploring different strategies that work better for you. Breaking out of old patterns can lead to new, more effective solutions.

The solution isn't necessarily related to the problem. The idea that the solution isn't directly tied to the problem is a fundamental shift in thinking. It encourages you to look for moments when the issue didn't occur—those unexpected times when you managed or coped in ways you may not have even noticed. These positive differences reveal solutions you're already using without needing to directly investigate the problem itself (Lutz 2013).

For instance, in relationships, instead of focusing on past disagreements, think back to a time when a small act of kindness or humor helped you reconnect after a conflict. Similarly, with anxiety, reflect on a moment when you felt the urge to avoid a challenging situation, yet you found yourself moving forward despite the fear. Maybe you dreaded going to a social event, but once you arrived and spoke with someone familiar, the anxiety began to lift.

These examples show how solutions can emerge from what's already working, even if it seems unrelated to the problem. Embracing this mindset may feel challenging at first, but it opens new ways to approach difficulties, making the path forward clearer.

The language for solutions differs from the language of problems. Talking about solutions shifts your focus from what's wrong to what's possible. A solution-focused mindset uses language that moves you toward your goals. By reflecting on actions that have already worked for you, you reshape your perspective and uncover solutions that are often already within your grasp.

It's possible to shift from a problem-focused to a solution-focused mindset. A mindset involves the actions you take, the relationships you nurture, and the language you use. Shifting to a solution-focused mindset allows you to focus on what you've already accomplished and what you aim to achieve. This shift empowers you to take meaningful steps forward with purpose.

The words you choose and the questions you ask can transform your mindset. By asking *What are my best hopes?* you open yourself to new possibilities. If you've had success before, you can do it again. A solution-focused mindset activates your resources, builds your agency, and inspires action. It's a mindset of hope, helping you recognize small victories and move forward with confidence.

Finding Joy in Everyday Moments

Joy is often found in the smallest moments of life. The weight of anxiety and depression may feel overwhelming for you, but by noticing simple pleasures—the warmth of sunlight on your skin or the quiet of a peaceful morning, you can gently turn your focus toward comfort. These moments offer a comforting reminder that joy is always within reach, even during challenging times.

This exercise guides you to reflect on these moments, helping you explore the joy woven into your everyday life. As you answer each question, ask yourself, *What else? Who else? How else? When else?* and *Where else?* As you do, you'll find a deeper appreciation for the world around you, nurturing a quiet contentment within.

Reflections on Moments of Joy

What did you most enjoy this past week? What were you doing during these moments that brought you joy?

____

____

____

____

____

How did these actions contribute to your happiness in those moments?

____

____

Who would notice you experiencing joy?

____

What would they most appreciate about seeing you in these moments of joy?

____

____

____

When did you first notice you were feeling joyful? What were you doing, noticing, or thinking at the time that helped you realize this feeling?

____

____

____

Where were you when these joyful moments occurred? How did your surroundings influence what you were doing to create or express joy?

____

____

____

How did you create these moments of joy? What intentional actions or choices did you make to bring about joy?

____

____

____

On a scale from 1–10, with 10 being very confident in your ability to intentionally create moments of joy in your life and 1 the opposite, what number would you give yourself?

____

What is a good enough number?

____

What keeps your number from being lower? What else?

____

____

What is one specific action you can take to increase your confidence in cultivating joy?

____

____

Spreading Joy

In everyday life, small moments—a shared laugh, a thoughtful gesture, or an act of kindness—often leave the most lasting impact. You might overlook them, thinking they are insignificant, but they brighten your day and others' in ways you might not even notice. This next exercise asks you to reflect on the times when you brought happiness, comfort, or pride to someone. Maybe you lent a helping hand, offered a smile, or simply listened when it was needed.

These actions, though simple, build deeper connections and foster trust. Take a moment to recall these experiences. As you reflect, you'll understand how these acts positively shape your relationships and help you contribute good to the world. In recognizing this, you'll also nurture your own growth.

As with prior exercises, ask yourself, *What else? Who else? How else? When else?* and *Where else?*

Reflections on Moments of Impact

What did you do this week that made someone laugh, feel better, or made a positive difference for them?

How did your actions make a difference to them?

Who noticed the effect of your actions? What would they say they appreciated most about what you did?

When did you realize you were having a positive impact on someone? What specific moment stood out to you?

____

____

Where were you when these interactions took place, and how did the environment influence your actions or the outcome?

____

____

How did these experiences benefit both you and the others involved?

____

____

How did you create these experiences? What choices or actions led you to cultivate these moments of joy or connection?

____

____

Reflecting on Personal Moments of Pride

In this exercise, you're invited to reflect on your accomplishments and moments of pride. In the midst of a busy world, personal victories can go unnoticed. Whether it's learning something new, helping a friend in need, or sticking to a goal you set, each action plays a role in shaping your journey. As you answer these questions, you'll reconnect with your strengths, appreciating the value of even the smallest moments. As with the previous exercises, ask yourself, *What else? Who else? How else? When else?* and *Where else?*

Embracing Your Proud Moments

What were you most proud of this week?

What specific actions did you take that made you feel proud?

Who would be most proud of your accomplishments?

What would they appreciate most about your success?

When did you realize you were experiencing pride and success? Was there a particular moment that stood out to you?

How was this experience of pride different from other times? How did it impact you?

____

____

____

____

____

How did you create these moments of pride and success?

____

____

____

____

____

____

Your Best Hopes for Reading This Book

Reflecting on the following questions is the first step toward aligning your journey with your best hopes. As you move forward, your desire to foster hope and create a meaningful plan will guide you. Your best hopes serve as the light that leads you toward positive change—each small step bringing you closer to the outcome you envision.

Take a moment to consider your desired outcome. These aspirations are the compass that will direct you, one step at a time, through each chapter as you build confidence in the life you're creating.

Best Hopes for This Book

Imagine your best hopes.

What are your best hopes, so that when you're finished reading this book, you can say it was worthwhile?

____

____

____

What would you be doing that would tell you it positively impacted your life?

____

____

____

Reflect on who would notice.

Who would notice when these changes happened?

____

What changes would they notice?

____

____

What would be different between you and those who would notice?

____

____

Evaluate your confidence level.

On a scale from 1–10, how confident are you that you'll do your best to try some of the exercises within this book?

____

What do you know about yourself that you'll do your best to try some of the exercises?

____

____

____

What keeps your number from being lower?

____

____

Plan your next steps forward.

What is one thing you could do to increase your number by one point?

____

____

How confident (from 1–10) are you that you'll do your best to take this one step? What keeps your number from being lower?

____

____

____

____

When you take a moment to reflect on these questions, you step toward aligning your actions with your deepest desires. Anxiety and depression might cloud your path, but your best hopes are always there to guide you. As you move through this book, pay attention to the effort you dedicate to growth, especially on days when progress feels frustratingly slow. The tools within these chapters offer practical ways to make those small shifts—whether by reaching out to someone for support when isolation sets in or practicing calming techniques when stress surfaces. Over time, these seemingly small actions can spark profound changes in your everyday life.

CHAPTER 2

Empower Your Story with Positive Language

Physicist Isidor Rabi, who won the Nobel Prize in 1944 for his work on magnetic resonance, said, "There are questions that illuminate and those that destroy. We should ask the first kind" (Feynman, Leighton, and Sands 1963, 171). Your questions are more than words; they are keys that unlock doors to new possibilities. Each one has the potential to spark curiosity, invite discovery, and lead you closer to your vision. With intention, you shape your reality, using language to bring solutions to light and to create progress. Questions ignite change, steering your thoughts and unveiling paths that lead to your success.

Your words breathe life into relationships, connecting you with loved ones, neighbors, children, and even the nature you care for. Language does more than exchange thoughts—it sparks connections, allowing you to be seen and understood. Whether you're chatting in person, texting, or writing, your words are stitching together the moments that define your relationships. Each conversation—big or small—ripples through your world, shaping the bonds that matter most.

But what happens when the language of anxiety and depression begin to take root in your mind? What shelter can you find when your mind feels trapped in a storm, with self-blame swirling and joy slipping away? Anxiety stirs relentlessly, depression pulls you down, and irritability crashes like a wave. These feelings seep into your thoughts, changing how you speak to yourself.

But suppose you change your questions? A new outlook can emerge—where despair fades, and in its place, you find strength. Self-criticism transforms into hopeful affirmations, lighting a path toward the calm you've been seeking. By reframing your questions, you can shift from despair to empowerment. Hope takes over where self-criticism once ruled, and the path to calm starts to unfold before you, giving you the strength to move forward.

The exercises in this chapter will guide you toward speaking solution-focused language naturally, equipping you to approach anxiety and depression with compassion. Imagine changing your mindset just by adjusting the questions you ask and the words you choose. You'll begin to foster a mindset filled with hope and possibility, transforming self-doubt into a source of strength. As your inner dialogue changes, your thoughts will gain the momentum to carry you toward your goals.

Changing Your Self-Talk

The most important conversation you have each day is the one you rarely speak aloud—your self-talk. This inner dialogue runs beneath the surface, subtly guiding your emotions, actions, and how you interact with the world. Positive self-talk can uplift you, providing strength to handle anxiety and depression, while negative self-talk chips away at your confidence. The good news is that you have the ability to rewrite that dialogue, creating a story that fosters empowerment and hope.

The Power of Positive Words

The words you use daily significantly impact your mental health. Words matter. Verbs matter. Adjectives matter. How you ask yourself questions matter. By asking yourself the right questions and using positive language, you have the power to transform your self-talk. Each shift toward words that reflect agency and optimism builds confidence and resilience. With every adjustment, you'll be better equipped to face challenges with clarity and determination.

Adopting positive words can shift your perspective, helping you address difficulties more optimistically and productively. As you examine the translations from problem-solving to solution-building words below, notice how solution-focused words convey greater confidence, action, and positive assumptions. Consider exploring how shifting from problem-focused to solution-focused language could influence your perspective. By reflecting on this change, you may notice a subtle yet impactful difference in your approach to challenges and daily experiences. This is an opportunity to see how altering your words can transform your mindset and actions.

Problem-Focused Words	Solution-Focused Translation
Problem	Challenge
Suffer	Endure
Mind wander	Mind wonder
Natural consequences	Learning opportunities
Why	You must have a good reason
Push	Encourage
Give up	Accept
Admit	Acknowledge

Consider the list of some positive words below. You can find a comprehensive list of positive words at the publisher's website for this book, http://www.newharbinger.com/54742.

Positive verbs: Advocate, appreciate, bear, care for, carry on, choose, conquer, cooperate, counsel, create, deal, decide, develop, discover, do, engage, figure out, forge on, guide, handle, hope, influence, join, know, lead, learn, manage, mentor, model, participate, persevere, persist, plan, play, realize, teach, tell, think, tolerate, trailblaze, try, want.

Positive adjectives: Adaptable, audacious, best, bold, brave, caring, concerned, confident, courageous, creative, daring, dedicated, determined, funny, good enough, gutsy, helpful, impressive, lovely, loving, most, passionate, patient, satisfied, strong, tenacious, thoughtful.

Choosing Words That Empower You

This exercise invites you to shift from problem-focused language to solution-focused language, offering a fresh way to navigate difficulties. By translating negative words with empowering alternatives, you'll reshape your perspective and responses. Use the list of positive verbs and adjectives above and in the online resources to help you develop fluency in solution-focused language. As you explore each scenario, substitute the negative term with its positive counterpart and reflect on how this new lens transforms your outlook. Ask yourself, *What else? How else? Who else? When else?* and *Where else?* to uncover deeper possibilities and insights as you progress.

Problem → Challenge

Take a moment to reflect on some of the problems you've recently encountered. Instead of seeing them as problems, try reframing them as challenges—opportunities for growth and learning. For example, instead of seeing a financial setback as a problem, you might view it as a challenge to improve your budgeting skills, seek advice, and an opportunity to chart a new economic road map. Notice how this subtle change in word choice can shift your perspective.

Imagine if you replaced every instance of "problem" in your vocabulary with "challenge." How might this shift in language transform your perspective and influence those around you? As you consciously embrace this change in wording, take a moment to reflect on these questions (either silently or on a separate sheet of paper):

- How did you deal with the challenge you faced?
- Who noticed how you faced this challenge?
- What did you learn from this challenge?
- Where did you get your strength to face this challenge?
- How well did you deal with this challenge from 1–10 (10 the best and 1 the opposite)?
- What keeps your number from being lower?
- What would be a good enough number?
- What is one thing you could do to increase your number?

Suffer → Endure

Instead of focusing on "suffering," consider embracing "enduring," a word that reflects your ability to adapt, confront challenges, and forge on with determination. While "suffering" can feel passive and overwhelming, "enduring" highlights your active role in navigating through tough times—how you've persevered, taking one step at a time to carve out a new direction.

For instance, rather than saying "I suffer from chronic stress," translate it to "I have endured tremendous stress and have remained steadfast in my desire to prevail." This change in language recognizes your strength and underscores the intentional actions you've taken to overcome obstacles:

- How did you endure the situation you faced?
- What strengths did you show while enduring this situation?
- How did this hardship build your resilience?
- Who supported you?
- Where did you find the strength to keeping moving forward?

Mistakes → Learning Opportunities

There are no mistakes—only learning opportunities. Consider a time when you made a swift decision to protect someone's feelings, only to disregard your own needs. Viewing this as a mistake might ignite guilt and frustration. For example, agreeing to tackle a task while feeling drained, just to prevent discomfort for someone else, could leave you feeling resentful and overwhelmed. When you label this situation as a "mistake," it often intensifies self-criticism and magnifies a sense of failure, focusing on what went wrong and amplifying the negative emotions that follow.

In contrast, suppose you name this situation as a learning opportunity—pausing to reflect on how avoiding difficult conversations to spare someone discomfort ultimately led to a situation where your own needs were neglected. Naming this experience as a learning opportunity (which develops skills to approach difficult conversations with courage instead of fear) transforms your perspective from one of failure to one of growth. Reframing your mistakes as valuable learning opportunities is a compassionate approach that soothes your stress response and creates space for change. This change in your language helps you moving forward to set clear boundaries and encourage honest dialogues, ultimately enriching your relationships and transforming setbacks into sources of confidence and clarity.

Reflect on a mistake you made and take a moment to appreciate how difficult this must have been for you. Instead of revisiting the specifics of the mistake, ask yourself the following questions:

- What did you learn from this experience?
- Who noticed that you used this as a learning opportunity?
- How did you apply this learning opportunity moving forward?
- What difference did it make to you and others?

Give Up → Accept

Acceptance encourages you to recognize your limits, forgive yourself, and continue with compassion. Unlike giving up, which feels like a final surrender, acceptance allows you to face challenges with understanding and self-compassion. By saying *I accept this is difficult,* you acknowledge the reality of the situation and create space to pause, reflect, and move forward with self-compassion. This shift in word choice helps you recognize that each small effort contributes to your growth, nurtured with kindness and gentleness.

Imagine a day when you wake up with the weight of depression, struggling to get out of bed. Instead of thinking, *I can't do this, I give up,* you pause and say, *I accept that today is difficult, but I can try one thing.* You decide to *start small*—maybe brushing your teeth or making breakfast. This shift recognizes the difficulty while allowing you to take manageable steps. Acceptance lets you acknowledge the struggle while still moving forward at your own pace, focusing on progress, however small.

Recall a moment when the weight of the situation felt overwhelming for you, pushing you to the edge of giving up. Reflect on the following questions:

- What helped you recognize it was time to pause and accept where you were?
- How did you realize it was time to accept the situation as it was?
- When did you feel ready to take this step toward acceptance?

- Where did you find the courage to accept your circumstances with kindness toward yourself?
- Who supported you during this process and appreciated your need to accept the situation? Was their support helpful for you, and if so, how was it helpful?

Daily focus. Each day, focus on one positive (solution-focused) word, replacing its negative (problem-focused) counterpart. By choosing positive words, you enhance your fluency in solution-focused language, reshaping your inner dialogue and nurturing a more optimistic outlook.

- Day 1—Challenge: Replace "problem" with "challenge" and say, *This is a challenge I can handle.*
- Day 2—Endure: Replace "suffer" with "endure" and remind yourself, *I have endured, and I have the strength to persevere.*
- Day 3—Learning Opportunity: Replace "mistake" with "learning opportunity" and think, *This is a valuable learning opportunity for me.*
- Day 4—Accept: Replace "give up" with "accept": *I accept that I'm having a hard time, and I appreciate that I'm doing the best I can.*

Reflect and expand. Reflect on how this shift in language has influenced your mood and perspective.

What difference did using positive words make?

____

____

____

____

____

____

How did these words impact your interactions?

___

___

___

Who noticed a change in your behavior?

___

Where did you find it easiest or hardest to use these words?

___

___

___

When did you feel most empowered by using positive language?

___

___

___

Cultivating a Positive Mindset Through Empowering Beliefs

Self-beliefs are the perceptions you hold about yourself, and they significantly influence your emotions and behaviors. Embracing positive assumptions about your abilities can transform your inner dialogue. For example, asking yourself, *Why do I feel so depressed and anxious?* can make those feelings worse. Conversely, asking, *What do I know about myself that shows I can overcome depression and anxiety?* can foster a sense of hope. Your self-beliefs shape your inner dialogue and impact how you navigate life's challenges. By learning to ask questions that recognize your potential, value your strengths, and affirm your worth, you'll build confidence in yourself.

Solution-focused language uses questions and statements that assume positive things about your capabilities, resources, and potential for change. This approach shapes your conversation by assuming favorable conditions are true, influencing how you interpret and respond. These assumptions shift your perspective, revealing your strength and ability to transform your life. Solution-focused questions are based on the belief that you *already have* the resources to live a fulfilling life and the capacity to endure adversity.

Let's explore how *starting* questions with one of these five simple words, combined with a positive belief, can significantly change how you think and feel about yourself, leading to new and more hopeful actions:

- *What* resources have you drawn on, even for small moments, to help you cope? Asking *what* assumes you have valuable resources to tap into.
- *How* have you been coping? *How* have you endured? Asking *how* assumes you have the resilience and ability to manage difficulties.
- *Who* are the most important people in your life? Asking *who* assumes that you have meaningful connections that uplift you.
- *When* did you last feel proud of yourself? Asking *when* assumes that you have accomplishments to be proud of.
- *Where* do you find your strength? Asking *where* assumes that you possess strength and can identify it.

By regularly asking yourself questions starting with these simple words, you can transform your inner dialogue, shift your mindset, and discover new ways to cope and thrive.

In the following exercise, you'll learn how to create empowering questions starting with one of these five simple words: what, how, who, where, and when. By combining each of these words with positive assumptions, you can shift your perspective and foster self-confidence.

Reflect on how embracing the positive assumptions listed below and starting questions with one of these five simple words (what, how, who, where, when) can impact your thinking. As you answer each question, ask yourself, *What else? How else? Who else? Where else?* and *When else?*

Cultivating a Positive Mindset

Positive Assumptions to Embrace:

You have the capacity to be kind and compassionate toward yourself and others.

You can recognize skills to mobilize your strengths.

You have the flexibility to adapt and switch directions when needed.

You can find emotional relief and cognitive clarity.

You can draw strength from your relationships.

You can function despite setbacks.

You can experience personal growth, including an enhanced appreciation for life.

You can recognize the importance of things you formerly took for granted.

You recognize and rediscover your personal strength.

You can see new possibilities for your life.

You can view aspects of your struggles and difficulties as potential gifts.

You can create a revised life narrative that can be a turning point.

You can experience greater spiritual and existential growth.

Let's use this positive assumption: *I have the capacity to be kind and compassionate toward myself and others.* Combine this assumption with the five simple words to create reflective questions.

What have you done to show kindness and compassion toward yourself and those around you?

___

___

___

How have you nurtured kindness and compassion toward yourself and others?

___

___

___

Who would notice the kindness and compassion you show to yourself and others?

___

___

___

Where have you found the strength to be kind and compassionate to yourself and others?

___

___

___

When have you most recently shown kindness and compassion to yourself?

___

___

___

Now it's your turn to practice crafting questions. Start by choosing one of the positive assumptions listed earlier in this exercise. Create your own solution-focused questions using words like what, how, who, where, and when. Consider how these questions help you uncover your strengths and build a more positive, resilient mindset.

You can repeat this process with other positive assumptions using a downloadable form at http://www.newharbinger.com/54742, where you'll also find a list of the top ten solution-focused questions.

Positive Assumption: ______________________________

____

____

What ______________________________?

____

____

____

____

____

How ______________________________?

____

____

____

____

____

Who ____?

____

____

____

____

____

Where ____?

____

____

____

____

____

When ____?

____

____

____

____

____

Using Questions—A Case Scenario

This case scenario will help you learn how to translate inner dialogues from one of despair to one of resilience and strength. We'll use the example of Elizabeth coping with the declining health of her husband, Carl, from progressive multiple sclerosis—a case we will revisit throughout this book.

Problem-Focused Inner Dialogue: The Weight of Despair

Elizabeth faces an overwhelming situation. Her husband, Carl, is experiencing a rapid decline in health and functioning due to progressive multiple sclerosis, a disease that worsens over time, leading to significant changes in their lives. Elizabeth juggles daily medical appointments for Carl, the stress of her job to support the family financially, and the responsibility of caregiving.

Elizabeth often wakes at 3 a.m. with anxiety and a sense of dread. Simple tasks like grocery shopping become solitary endeavors, as Carl lacks the strength to accompany her. Each day feels like a never-ending cycle of isolated chores, with no relief in sight. The unpredictability of their situation fuels her need for control, increasing her irritability and underlying feelings of fear and depression. Guilt and self-blame consume her, making her feel more irritable and depressed. She constantly feels she should do more and work harder to support his growing needs and care for their family, making joy seem distant and unattainable.

The future may seem grim for Carl and Elizabeth; yet even in the face of such overwhelming news, pathways to resilience and agency exist. Shifting focus to areas within your control can reveal opportunities to live with intention and meaning. One such technique is giving appreciation.

Appreciative observations focus on recognizing and valuing the positive qualities and strengths demonstrated by individuals facing challenges. To identify these observations, Carl can ask the question, *What do I most appreciate about Elizabeth?* This question helps draw out specific traits and actions that reflect resilience, dedication, and other admirable qualities. Each appreciative observation is followed by a question starting with what, how, who, when, or where. These questions can be expanded using *What else? How else? Who else? Where else?* and *When else?*

Trait/Behavior	Observation	Question
Resilience in handling responsibilities	Elizabeth manages a complex array of duties, including Carl's medical appointments, her job, and caregiving responsibilities, showing remarkable strength and determination despite the overwhelming circumstances.	How does she sustain her strength and resilience while juggling these demanding roles, and what does she do to recharge?
Dedication to family support	Her commitment to supporting Carl through his progressive illness and ensuring the financial stability of her family highlights her unwavering devotion and love.	Where does she find the strength to remain steadfast in her support for Carl while balancing her own well-being and the responsibilities for her family?
Acknowledgment of personal challenges	Despite feeling overwhelmed and struggling with anxiety, Elizabeth recognizes her emotional struggles, reflecting her self-awareness and honesty about her difficulties.	How has she managed to acknowledge and face her emotional challenges with such honesty, and what support systems or self-care strategies has she found helpful?
Guilt and self-blame	Although guilt and self-blame consume her, it underscores her deep concern for Carl's well-being and her strong sense of responsibility, revealing her caring nature.	How has she managed the guilt and self-blame while also prioritizing her own self-care?
Efforts to provide financial support	Her stress over balancing a job while caregiving highlights her commitment to ensuring financial stability for her family, reflecting her dedication and hard work.	Who has supported her in balancing her job and caregiving responsibilities, and how has their support impacted her ability to also care for herself?
Endurance	Her ability to endure a cycle of isolated chores and relentless daily demands shows her remarkable endurance and resilience under difficult circumstances.	Where does she find the motivation to keep going through the daily demands she faces, and how does she ensure that she is caring for her own needs as well?

Elizabeth's Transformed Narrative of Resilience

Elizabeth made a conscious choice to focus on recognizing their daily successes and sources of joy. Together with Carl, they identified moments of joy and celebrated small victories. They found comfort in their beloved dogs, enjoyed their meals together, connected with their children through heartwarming Zoom calls, and discovered new places like a delightful Korean restaurant and a local grocery store with homemade soups.

Their approach included daily check-ins to discuss how well they were managing their mental load and coping with challenges. They labeled their experiences humorously as "optimistic," "nihilistic," or "hedonistic" to acknowledge their feelings nonjudgmentally. This practice helped them shift their perspectives, find comfort, and uncover moments of joy even within their difficult circumstances.

By asking herself the transformative questions, Elizabeth began to see her strengths and resilience. She recognized her capacity to manage multiple responsibilities and appreciated the support from those around her. She discovered that her determination and ability to find joy in small moments were powerful tools for coping with their situation.

Elizabeth's narrative shifted from one of despair to one of resilience. She cultivated her resources, rediscovered her strengths, and found ways to sustain herself moving forward. By focusing on what she could appreciate and celebrate, Elizabeth transformed her inner dialogue and embraced a solution-focused mindset that empowered her to navigate life's challenges with grace and hope.

By applying this exercise, you can transform your narrative by reflecting on compliments and what you appreciate about yourself. Recognizing your positive assumptions and combining them with these five simple questions will help shift your perspective, empowering you to find resilience and strength in difficult situations

Appreciative Reflections

What do you most appreciate about yourself?

What are you most proud of?

Who do you most appreciate? What would they say they most appreciate about you?

List all the positive words that you discovered through these questions.

Now, using the appreciative observations you've identified, develop your own questions. Remember to expand your inquiry by asking *What else? How else? Who else? Where else?* and *When else?* to explore deeper layers of meaning. Let's walk through an example using "compassion" as an identified strength. Notice how you can frame solution-focused questions that prompt reflection and insight:

- What moments reveal your compassion most clearly? What else could you do to show it more often?
- How has your compassion made a difference in someone's life? How else can you apply it to new challenges?
- Who benefits most from your compassionate nature? Who else could you support with this strength?
- Where do you feel your compassion is most needed? Where else could it have a profound impact?
- When has your compassion been most appreciated? When else can you offer it to others in unexpected ways?

Consider everything you've uncovered through this reflection. What steps can you take now to harness and amplify your strengths?

____

____

____

____

____

____

____

____

Clarity Through Languaging: Transforming Your Words into Action

Solution-focused language is both simple and powerful: if something works, do more of it; if it doesn't, try something different. The key is the verb *do*. Languaging, introduced by Harlene Anderson, involves defining the meaning of your words and identifying the verbs that guide your actions (Anderson and Goolishian 1992). This process translates your thoughts and emotions into actionable steps. While acknowledging your feelings is important, it's often not enough to drive progress. Shifting from passive expressions to proactive, solution-focused language reclaims your agency and empowers you to tackle challenges decisively.

Language often conceals more than it reveals, leading to confusion and misunderstanding. When we rely on vague, problem-centered words, we strip ourselves of the power to act. This is where the power of positive language, discussed earlier, comes into play. By intentionally using words that are positive and convey action, you regain control over how you see the world. The transformation is profound. Words, which can be tools of ambiguity, become instruments of clarity and empowerment. No longer just descriptive, they invite action and change.

Let's explore an example to help you understand. Ask yourself what it means to get through your day. Take a moment to consider: What does getting through your day mean to you? Who *would notice* when you have gotten through your day? What *did you do* when you got through your day? Your answers reveal your personal solutions.

Words like "happy," "joyful," and "at peace" may seem positive, but they often lack clarity because they hold different meanings for each person. What does "happy" truly look like for you? How does "joyful" show up in your daily routine?

This is where the power of precise language comes in. What do you actually do when you're feeling joyful? How do you act when you're at peace? Defining these actions brings those feelings to life and guides you toward making them a reality.

To dig deeper, ask yourself (and answer in your head):

- What do "happy," "joyful," and "at peace" truly mean to you?
- When you felt these emotions, what specific actions did you take?
- How did you intentionally create these moments of happiness, joy, or peace?
- Who notices when you're experiencing these emotions? What would they see you doing?
- Where were you during those pleasant moments?

These questions help you move beyond vague terms and identify the actions that make a real difference in your life. By breaking down these moments, you can uncover your unique, actionable verbs—steps that are tied to your experiences. To explore even further, use prompts like *What else? How else? Who else? Where else?* and *When else?* to deepen your understanding and craft a realistic plan, one step at a time.

Doing Instead: Turning Negative Thoughts into Positive Action

Fluency in solution-focused language can feel elusive when you're grappling with depression and anxiety. Problem-focused thinking often becomes the default—familiar, ingrained, and difficult to shake. It fills your mind with negative words and powerless verbs, leaving you feeling stuck. You might find that when asked about your daily hopes, the only response you can muster is a desire to escape the suffocating gloom or outrun the rising panic. These emotions are intense, and it's important to recognize and validate them. But after doing so, ask yourself a pivotal question: What would you be doing instead?

Navigating choices while pursuing a healthier lifestyle can be challenging, such as when you're tempted by a second piece of cake. Simply telling yourself "Don't eat the cake" often amplifies the craving. Instead, consider what actions you've taken in the past when you managed to resist. Think about the moments when you successfully chose not to indulge. What strategies did you use? How did avoiding the cake positively impact you? Reflect on what you told yourself to stay committed and who supported your decision.

By focusing on what you've done instead, such as enjoying a cup of tea, diving into a book, doing quick stretches, or looking forward to social events, you reveal a range of effective alternatives. Life is full of decisions and trade-offs. Embracing this perspective allows you to make empowered choices, transforming how you handle challenges.

Uncovering your root verbs—the fundamental actions that define your accomplishments and aspirations—is essential for meaningful change. While this process might initially seem to slow you down, it paradoxically accelerates your progress. Essentially, defining your verbs provides a clearer road map, making it easier and faster to move forward with purpose.

Naming Your Verbs and Doing Instead

This exercise will guide you from problem-focused (negative) self-talk to solution-focused (actionable) steps. The goal is to identify and use verbs—what you do—to create positive changes in your life.

Reflect on your best hopes. Begin by asking yourself: What are your best hopes for the upcoming week? Perhaps it is feeling at peace or confident. Maybe your hopes are expressed in negative terms—such as "not feeling depressed," "not being financially strapped," or "not being stuck in the same job"—write down whatever comes to mind.

____

____

____

____

Reframe your hopes into positive language. If you answered with problem-focused language (not feeling depressed, not being financially strapped, or not being stuck in the same job), translate them to positive language by asking yourself the "doing instead" question: *Suppose I was not financially strapped, not feeling depressed, and not being stuck in the same job—what would I be doing instead*? This question helps translate your hopes into actionable steps and activates your sense of agency.

Clarify the meaning of your positive words. Once you get to a positive word, now it's time to define what it means to you by asking yourself this simple question. What do you mean by (e.g., at peace or confident)?

____

____

____

____

Translate your positive words into verbs. Now it's time to turn your positive words into concrete actions. Ask yourself the following questions and remember you can deepen this exploration with *What else? How else? Who else? Where else?* and *When else?* For example, if your positive word is "confident," consider these questions:

When did you last feel confident? What were you doing at that time?

Who would notice when you're confident? What did they see you doing?

How did you create those moments of confidence?

Identify your verbs. From your reflections, identify the actions you took—your personalized verbs. List your verbs, as they represent what you do when you feel better.

Reflect further. When have you done those things? How did you make them happen? How did you stay motivated? When did you find time for them? How did you plan them?

Create an action plan. Using the verbs you identified, write down specific actions you can take today, tomorrow, and this week.

Scale your confidence. On a scale from 1–10, where 10 means you're very confident you'll do one of your named verbs and 1 means the opposite, rate your current confidence. What gives you this confidence?

____

____

____

____

What keeps your number from being lower?

____

____

____

Transforming "If Only" into Action

Sometimes, you might find yourself trapped in a negative mindset, feeling overwhelmed by thoughts that make you feel powerless. For example, you might wish for more appreciation from your boss, hope for less divisiveness in the world, or yearn for a better work environment. These "if only" thoughts can leave you feeling stuck.

Take a moment to jot down two of your "if only" thoughts:

1. ____

2. ____

To shift from this feeling of helplessness, use presuppositional language—that is, assume that you already know what to do. This technique involves framing your thoughts with positive assumptions about success or outcomes. By first acknowledging your situation and then shifting your focus to actionable steps, you validate your experience while encouraging practical action.

Reflect on your "if only" scenarios. For example, if you're dealing with a difficult situation, ask yourself: "If only [X] weren't happening, what would I be doing instead?" This approach validates your concern but directs your attention to possible actions.

Consider these questions to explore your actions:

- What else would you be doing?
- When have you been able to do this?
- How did you make it happen?

Apply this method to your own scenarios. Write down your questions using the format: "If only [X] were different, what would I be doing?"

____

____

____

____

____

____

____

____

____

By turning your "if only" thoughts into practical actions, you can empower yourself to make a positive difference that is within your control.

When you put all of these strategies together, you can shift your narrative from despair to hope. Carl's story illustrates how to use positive words, verbs, beliefs, and questions to transform negative self-talk into action.

Climbing Higher Instead of Digging Deeper: The Case of Carl

Carl was struggling with depression as he was dealing with facing daily challenges and frustrations of multiple sclerosis. From spilling butter to struggling in physical therapy, it all added up to a feeling of hopelessness. Let's take a look at a few challenges Carl faced and how he used the tools in this chapter to see his situation differently.

Physical Therapy Session

Negative self-talk: "When my physical therapist mentioned that I might be getting weaker, I felt like I was lazy and a failure. No matter what I do, it just gets worse. Why continue? Maybe it's all a waste of time."

Appreciation and compliments:

Dedication: You show incredible dedication by continuing with physical therapy.

Courage: Your willingness to face daily challenges with courage is remarkable.

Questions to transform the narrative:

What motivates you to keep attending your physical therapy sessions?

How have you shown courage and dedication in facing your condition's challenges?

Who in your support team helps you brainstorm and find new ways to manage better?

Where do you find the strength to keep going despite your disease's unpredictability?

When have you experienced moments of resilience and perseverance in your journey?

Solution-focused perspective: "I understand that I might be getting weaker, but I'll keep doing my best in physical therapy to maintain my health and strength. Despite the unpredictable nature of this disease, I am dedicated to making it to all my appointments and courageously facing the challenges."

Spilled Butter Incident

Negative self-talk: "I spilled the butter because I left it in the microwave too long. I feel so stupid for making such a mistake. Now I have to clean it up, and it feels like everything I do ends up in a mess. I feel like I don't contribute to the family and that I'm just a burden to them."

Appreciation and compliments:

Responsibility: You recognized the mistake and took action to correct it.

Determination: Despite the intense fatigue from MS, you manage daily tasks. This perseverance is impressive.

Endurance: The exhaustion you feel is immense, yet you still do your best each day.

Self-awareness: You're conscious of your actions and their impact.

Contributions: Your efforts, presence, and resilience significantly contribute to your family.

Questions to transform the narrative:

What strengths did you demonstrate by taking responsibility for your actions?

How have you kept going despite feeling deeply exhausted?

Who in your family appreciates your effort, and how have they shown support?

Where can you find small moments of rest to help manage your fatigue?

When have you handled similar challenges successfully, and what did you learn?

Solution-focused perspective: "I recognize that even small tasks can be monumental with MS. Despite feeling utterly exhausted, I managed to handle the situation, showing my strength and determination. Watching my loyal dog lick up the mess on the floor brought a smile to my face. As I bent down to clean, it became a moment of movement for me, what my physical therapists call a 'movement snack.'"

Socializing with Friends and Family

Negative self-talk: "I don't want to spend time with friends and family because they'll pity me. It's hard for them to watch me struggle to walk, and I feel embarrassed about how I look."

Compliments and appreciation:

Good listener: You're a good listener and are genuinely curious about others.

Determination: Your family and friends value your determination and strength.

Questions to transform the narrative:

What do your friends and family appreciate most about your presence?

How have you shown determination and strength in your interactions?

Who among your friends and family has shown the most support, and how?

Where do you feel most comfortable and valued with loved ones?

When have you experienced meaningful and supportive interactions?

Solution-focused perspective: "When I let myself be with friends and family, I discovered how supportive and helpful they are. I am a good listener, and my family and friends appreciate our conversations. These moments hold the true essence of life, and I cherish them, knowing that time is precious and it's important to savor every moment."

Transforming Your Own Narrative

Reflect on your own challenges: Identify what you appreciate about yourself. Write down the qualities and actions you admire, respect, and value and use the five simple words to ask reflective questions:

What strengths have you shown in managing your challenges?

What does your ability to acknowledge your feelings say about your resilience?

How have you demonstrated dedication and perseverance in difficult times?

How has being open about your struggles contributed to your personal growth?

Who have you relied on for support, and how has that impacted you?

Who benefits from your efforts and care, and in what ways?

Where have you found the strength to keep going despite your challenges?

Where have you shown empathy and compassion in your life?

When have you experienced moments of personal growth or joy despite difficulties?

When did you first recognize your need for self-care, and how did you respond?

In this chapter, you have explored exercises to transform negative self-talk into positive, action-oriented steps using solution-focused language. By incorporating positive words, verbs, beliefs, and empowering questions, you have learned to shift your narrative from despair to hope and resilience.

In the next chapter, you'll learn to calm your mind and alleviate the distress of depression and anxiety using solution-focused tools.

CHAPTER 3

Become an Amygdala Whisperer: Managing Intense Emotions with Compassion

Emotions are powerful signals, guiding you toward what nurtures you and away from what depletes you. They offer insight into what is working in your life and what may require change. By pausing to acknowledge and name your emotions, you gain clarity on what you truly need, what actions would support your well-being, and where boundaries may need to be established to protect you. While it's not always easy, being able to feel and acknowledge these emotions is a gift—they help you pause, reflect, and recalibrate. Without these signals, navigating life's challenges or recognizing opportunities for growth would be far more difficult.

Amygdala whispering is the art of soothing your emotional storms by speaking to yourself with empathy. The term amygdala whispering is inspired by horse whispering, a method of calming and training horses by quietly talking to them and observing their nonverbal cues. This concept dates back to the nineteenth century when an Irish horseman named Daniel "Horse-Whisperer" Sullivan gained fame in England for rehabilitating horses that had become vicious and unmanageable due to abuse or accidental trauma (Powell 1872).

Similarly, amygdala whispering involves observing your thoughts, feelings, and actions to understand what you need. Amygdala whispering focuses on comforting and calming yourself through self-compassion and self-care. It involves observing, tolerating, and affirming your emotions to clarify your needs and take steps to meet them. Acknowledging your experience with kindness can gently guide you back to a calmer state.

Your communication patterns and behaviors can signal whether you're calm or experiencing a stress response. Staying attuned to these cues helps you identify your needs and act compassionately. In this chapter, you'll discover compassionate, solution-focused tools to help you recognize and manage your emotions with empathy and clarity. However, before diving into this chapter on managing dysregulation, you might find it useful to gauge your overall well-being with the wellness evaluation exercise at http://www.newharbinger.com/54742.

Understanding Your Brain

Your brain is a masterpiece of interconnected parts: the amygdala, hippocampus, and prefrontal cortex. These structures work together to help you adapt to stress, stay calm, think clearly, and make good decisions when feeling overwhelmed, anxious, or stuck in negative thoughts (Kemeny 2009).

The amygdala acts like an alarm system, quickly detecting emotions (like fear and excitement) and triggering fast reactions (such as jumping back when you see a snake). The prefrontal cortex helps you think things through and make decisions, allowing you to manage and control your emotions more calmly. For instance, it helps you stay calm and realize the snake is behind glass at a zoo, so there's no need to be scared. The hippocampus plays a crucial role in forming and storing memories, including emotional ones, helping you remember past experiences and influencing your reactions to new situations.

Together, the amygdala, prefrontal cortex, and hippocampus balance your responses, helping you feel safer and more empowered during stressful moments by drawing on both immediate emotional triggers and past experiences.

The Basement of Your Brain

The amygdala, deep within your brain, is a small, almond-shaped structure crucial for emotions. Think of it as your brain's basement alarm system, triggering the fight-flight-or-freeze response to prepare your body to react by either running away or defending yourself.

In short, the amygdala detects emotions, triggers quick reactions, and stores emotional memories, especially those related to fear and excitement. When you encounter a stressful situation that feels beyond your control, the amygdala springs into action, heightening your alertness. This activation sends you straight into the basement of your brain, where instinct takes over with automatic responses: fight, flight, or freeze.

Faced with danger, your amygdala doesn't deliberate; it reacts. Suddenly, you're in survival mode, where rational thought takes a back seat. Emotions erupt, and your ability to remain composed wanes. Clear thinking feels distant, overshadowed by a rush of urgency that clouds your usual calm. Here, emotions overwhelm, making it harder to access the steady, measured responses you need. In this basement state, joy slips away and the ability to connect with others fades. Finding clarity in your words proves arduous, while quieting the rush poses a steep upward climb.

These intense emotional states, or *amygdala storms*, describe the mental chaos that happens when you experience a loss of agency and choice. In these high-stress moments, your brain reacts as if you're in a storm, making it hard to think clearly or see your options. Just as a snowstorm blinds you or a sandstorm makes it impossible to see, these internal storms block your ability to process thoughts, leaving you feeling trapped.

Depression and anxiety can trigger your body's fight-flight-or-freeze response, churning beneath the surface, yet invisible to others. Unlike a physical injury, these conditions manifest through changes in mood, behavior, or energy that can be difficult for outsiders to detect. These conditions can push you into a reactive state, where you're no longer grounded in the present but instead caught in a cycle of fear, dread, or hopelessness. Understanding how depression and anxiety co-opt your automatic responses helps reveal why these conditions feel so consuming—because they are, at their core, driving your body and mind into survival overdrive.

Below are signals you might notice when you're in survival mode—whether it's being thrown in the basement, caught in trauma fever, stuck in a brain blizzard, or blinded by a haboob. These signs are a natural part of how your body and mind respond to a perceived or real loss of agency. It's the nervous system's way of signaling stress, each reaction serving as a reminder that something deeper is at play. Pay attention to these cues—they reveal how your system is coping. By doing so, you reclaim your agency—recognizing your power to make choices, assert your needs, and rise above survival mode with clear intention.

Fight Response:

- Irritability and anger: easily frustrated or angry at small things, snapping at people, or frequently arguing
- Defensiveness: feeling the need to justify yourself or feeling attacked by mild criticism
- Hypervigilance: being constantly on edge, looking out for potential threats, can be exhausting and make it hard to relax or focus
- Aggressive behavior: aggressive outbursts are a way to assert control over your environment
- Protecting others: confronting perceived threats head-on to safeguard loved ones, like a parent fiercely protecting their child

Flight Response:

- Withdrawal: isolating yourself from social interactions and activities you once enjoyed to avoid further stress or disappointment
- Avoidance: avoiding situations that could cause additional stress, such as procrastinating on tasks or skipping important appointments
- Numbing: emotional and physical detachment that leads to a sense of emptiness or indifference—people experiencing numbing feel "shut down," where emotions are muted, making them feel disconnected from life's events and interactions
- Dissociation: disconnection from reality or from one's own thoughts, body, or surroundings—it can feel like being outside your body or detached from the world, and it ranges from mild states like daydreaming to more severe experiences, such as losing memory or feeling disconnected from one's identity
- People-pleasing: engaging in behaviors to prevent conflict and maintain peace, often neglecting your needs

Freeze Response:

- Freeze—becoming motionless in response to fear or threat, with the body pausing all movement to avoid detection or harm
- Stiffen—tensing up the muscles without movement, preparing for potential danger
- Hold—maintaining breath or posture without change, often unconsciously
- Stop—abruptly halting actions or movement in response to fear
- Lock —muscles or joints become immobile, as if frozen in place
- Brace—tensing the body in anticipation of impact or danger

Amygdala storms are a natural response to being pushed past your limits. Your body instinctively reacts to protect you, even if it clouds your judgment. Naming your experience is the first act of self-compassion—it anchors you on the path to reclaiming your agency. Each moment of recognition, affirmation, or self-questioning becomes a deliberate step, moving you away from the chaos and turbulence of emotional storms. When you do this, it opens the door to asking yourself a crucial question: *What do I need right now?* This simple, compassionate inquiry can guide you toward meeting your immediate emotional needs.

Climbing Upstairs to Your Prefrontal Cortex

The prefrontal cortex, located just behind your forehead, is the upstairs of your brain. It's where you manage emotions, make decisions, and plan for the future. When you face a challenge, this part of your brain allows you to break down tasks and strategize step by step. Instead of avoiding initiating a daunting project, your prefrontal cortex helps you analyze, prioritize, and act with intention. It's the voice of reason during difficult conversations, the force that helps you sort through emotions when anxiety starts creeping in.

But there's more to this process. The act of questioning yourself, especially with solution-focused questions, is like a mental workout for the prefrontal cortex, training it to stay strong and engaged. These questions—such as *What's one small step I can take right now?* or *How have I navigated similar challenges before?*—are not just answers you seek. They're mental tools that anchor you upstairs, keeping you from being dragged down into the reactive basement where fear and panic reign.

Each question you ask is like a lifeline, pulling you out of survival mode. They activate your ability to choose, showing you that you have options beyond fight, flight, or freeze. These questions don't just help you survive; they allow you to navigate with clarity and regain your sense of agency. As you continue engaging your brain this way, you gain mastery; being grounded and flexible, enabling you to face whatever comes next with confidence and resilience. Through this process, you regain hope by realizing you always have options and the ability to create a path forward, no matter the challenge.

Activities Indicating Prefrontal Cortex Activation

- Planning: creating a detailed schedule or road map for a project
- Organizing: structuring tasks or environments systematically
- Analyzing: evaluating information critically to make informed decisions
- Prioritizing: determining the importance of tasks and arranging them accordingly
- Decision-making: making thoughtful and deliberate choices

- Reflecting: thinking back on past experiences to learn and improve
- Strategizing: developing long-term plans to achieve goals
- Focusing: maintaining concentration on a single task without getting distracted
- Judging: assessing situations to form balanced opinions
- Inhibiting: controlling impulses and resisting distractions
- Reasoning: using logic to understand and solve problems
- Coordinating: harmonizing different elements of a task to work together effectively
- Innovating: coming up with new ideas and creative solutions
- Regulating emotions: managing your emotional responses to stay calm and focused

These actions and activities show that you're engaging the upstairs of your brain, effectively using your prefrontal cortex to think clearly, solve problems, make decisions, and manage your emotions.

Reclaiming Agency and Building a Path Forward

In moments of danger or perceived threat, when it feels like your control has slipped away, the solution-focused approach offers a compassionate way to calm your inner storm—amygdala whispering. Danger can be understood as a state of feeling powerless, where you lack both agency and a plan. When you don't feel like you have the ability to make choices or influence your situation, your brain interprets this as a threat. The fight-flight-or-freeze response takes over, plunging you into survival mode—into the basement of your brain, where fear, panic, and reactive instincts dominate.

On the other hand, hope is built on agency and having a plan. When you recognize your power to make decisions, even small ones, and you have a clear direction, you move out of the storm. By taking action, you climb upstairs from the reactive basement into the calmer, more deliberate part of your brain where you can think clearly. The solution-focused approach offers practical, action-oriented tools to help you reclaim your agency. Through specific questions, you're guided to recognize what you have done, are doing, and can do—right now. These questions aren't just for finding answers—they're linguistic tools that activate your ability to choose, act, and move forward. Each small action restores your agency, and with each step, you regain clarity—calming your amygdala storm. You're no longer stuck in survival mode; instead, you're making deliberate decisions with a plan in place.

When danger feels as though everything is slipping beyond your reach, hope arises from recognizing the steps you've already taken, even those you might have overlooked. By acknowledging your past and present actions, you begin to ignite the momentum to move forward. This realization fuels your ability to make decisions and reclaim your path, shifting you from uncertainty to a place of empowered action, where each step strengthens your resolve and confidence in navigating challenges ahead.

Recognizing Amygdala Storms and Making a Plan

Imagine facing a situation where you feel powerless, like Luiza, a mother torn between her sick child and the pressure to maintain her job. Ana has a fever, and the financial burden of missing work hangs heavily over Luiza's head. Her mind spins as she juggles the fever thermometer in one hand and her phone in the other, responding to urgent emails. She feels paralyzed, uncertain whether to comfort her child or answer her boss. She begins to feel a sense of panic as stress floods her system—her thoughts scatter, her heartbeat quickens—her brain's fight-flight-or-freeze response triggered by the perceived lack of agency. In that moment, her world feels out of control, and she's plunged into survival mode, navigating pure instinct, desperate for a way out of the chaos.

But then, through small, deliberate steps, Luiza reclaims her agency. Hope returns when she pauses, reflects, and advocates for her needs. She realizes she managed a similar situation before where she asked for help—from family, friends, and her workplace. She negotiated with her employer to work from home, explaining her situation with assertiveness. At home, she reached out to a close friend, asking them to help share the burden of childcare.

The following guided exercise uses the example of Luiza to help you reflect on moments in your life when you've felt overwhelmed, stuck in reactive thinking, or trapped by a lack of choices. You'll learn to recognize when you've lost your sense of agency and how to actively reclaim it.

Keep in mind the familiar questions we've discussed throughout this book—questions that guide you toward clearer solutions—*What else? How else? Who else? When else? Where else?* Reflect on these as you work through the process. These prompts allow you to explore beyond the obvious and discover deeper, more effective answers.

Managing Amygdala Storms

Actions in Different States

What do you do when you're upstairs (calm, clear-thinking)?

____

____

____

Example: *Luiza recognizes she needs to both care for Ana and fulfill work obligations. While upstairs, she plans, breaking tasks into manageable steps: she schedules work calls during the child's nap, arranges backup childcare, and calmly communicates with her boss.*

What do you do when you're downstairs (in survival mode)?

____

____

____

Example: *Luiza panics and becomes overwhelmed, jumping between caring for Ana and trying to meet work demands without any structure. She snaps at Ana or feels paralyzed, unable to complete either task effectively.*

Who would notice when you're upstairs or downstairs? What would they notice you doing?

____

____

____

____

____

Example:

- *When her mom is upstairs, Ana notices how much more present and attentive Luiza is. Ana feels her mother's gentle words and focused care, whether reading stories, playing games, or ensuring she is resting comfortably. However, when her mom is downstairs, Ana becomes clingier and irritable. She senses her mother's frustration and distraction. Instead of feeling reassured, Ana picks up on her mother's anxiety and emotional distance, leaving her unsettled.*
- *Her coworkers recognize when Luiza's in her upstairs state by the way she responds promptly to emails with thoughtful, friendly messages. Her ability to stay focused and prioritize tasks makes her seem steady and reliable. However, when she's in the downstairs state, they notice she easily becomes scattered. Deadlines get missed, and her responses to messages become short and curt.*
- *Her partner can tell when she's upstairs through her steady demeanor. Instead of handling everything alone, she reaches out for help, her voice calm as she sets boundaries and shares responsibilities. Her actions create a sense of teamwork. Downstairs, it's different. Frustration tightens her tone—short, clipped responses take over, leaving her partner at a distance. She withdraws. She shoulders the burden herself, stress amplifying as she struggles to manage everything alone.*

Recognizing States

When have you been able to recognize that you're upstairs or downstairs?

____

____

____

____

Example: *Luiza begins to recognize she's downstairs when she feels trapped—her thoughts race, her chest tightens, and she can't focus on any one task. She realizes she's upstairs when she feels calm, laying out a plan for work, organizing her child's care, and setting boundaries with her boss.*

Was it helpful for you to recognize where you are, and if so, how was it helpful?

____

____

____

____

____

Example: *Yes, it was helpful. When Luiza realizes she's downstairs, she pauses. She quietly asks herself,* What do I need right now? *This simple question pulls her back from spiraling into worst-case thoughts, grounding her in the present. She reflects on what's worked before. By focusing on what she can do and accepting what's beyond her reach, Luiza regains a sense of agency. She feels calmer, able to approach the day with more clarity, bringing a little peace to both herself and her child.*

How were you able to recognize those states?

____

____

____

____

____

Example: *For Luiza, physical signs like a racing heart or shallow breathing signal she's in the basement. Her thoughts are scattered and filled with fear*: I can't do this. What if I lose my job?

When she's upstairs, her inner dialogue shifts. She asks herself questions like How have I handled this before? *and* What did I accomplish today? *With clear, practical steps*—I'll email my boss for flexibility, and ask my partner to help with dinner—*her mind becomes focused and steady. Her breathing slows, and she can think critically and make deliberate decisions.*

Calming Strategies

Have you always been able to calm your storms, or is this different for you? If it is different, how is it different?

____

____

____

____

____

Example: *Yes—for Luiza this is different. In the past, she would immediately go into panic mode. This frantic state left her feeling helpless, unable to make clear decisions. When Luiza shifted into her upstairs mindset, she began asking herself thoughtful questions*—How have I handled this before? *As she reflected, she noticed solutions she'd previously overlooked.*

- *By setting up a comfort station near her workspace, she found a way to keep her child close and comfortable while resting.*
- *She established a work-and-play schedule, giving her child clarity about when she'd be available.*
- *Luiza also created a child-friendly workspace, offering activities like coloring or educational games to keep her child engaged while she worked.*
- *Simplifying meals, by prepping in advance or using delivery, reduced stress.*

These small adjustments allowed her to find balance she hadn't realized was possible.

Self-Assessment

On a scale from 1–10, where are you now in your ability to calm your amygdala storms?

____

Example: *Luiza rates herself a 5.*

What would be a good enough number? What would you be doing at this good enough number?

___

___

Example: *Luiza's good enough number would be a 7. At that number, she could remain present with her child, handling both caregiving and work with greater ease.*

What keeps your number from being lower? What else have you done to keep it from being lower?

___

___

___

___

___

Example: *When she feels herself heading toward the basement, Luiza pauses and acknowledges that this is a difficult situation. She asks,* How have I handled situations like this before? What have I accomplished today, and what do I need right now to make this good enough? *These brief moments of reflection help her stay present and calm the storm enough to be there for herself and her child.*

What is one thing you could do to increase your number?

___

___

___

Upstairs One Step at a Time

After reflecting on her experience, Luiza put together an action plan to help her climb upstairs out of an amygdala storm:

1. Pause and breathe. When Luiza feels herself heading downstairs, she will pause and take slow, deep breaths. This helps her shift from panic to presence.
2. Acknowledge the situation. She will affirm that the situation is challenging, giving herself permission to feel the weight of it without judgment.
3. Ask key questions:

What do I need right now to make this more tolerable?

What have I already done to manage this?

How have I handled similar situations in the past?

4. Reflect on what's important. Luiza will remind herself of meaningful moments even during difficult times.
5. Communicate and delegate. Luiza will reach out to people to let them know her needs and how they can help.
6. Stay present. Throughout the day, she will periodically pause to breathe, reflect, and adjust as needed, staying grounded in the present moment.
7. Recognize progress. At the end of the day, she will acknowledge the steps she took to regain agency, recognizing her ability to manage both her emotions and her responsibilities.

By following this plan, Luiza will feel more confident in her ability to climb back upstairs, one step at a time, while creating space for both herself and her child to find peace amid the storm.

When following this basic action plan isn't enough to get you from downstairs to upstairs, self-empathy can also help you self-soothe.

Embracing Self-Empathy

Empathy is the ability to understand and share the feelings of another person. It involves not just recognizing the emotions someone else is experiencing, but also feeling with them, placing yourself in their emotional world. This skill requires both cognitive and emotional processes—understanding another person's perspective and emotionally connecting with their experience. Self-empathy and empathy for others share the common thread of understanding and recognizing emotions, but they differ significantly in application. While empathy for others involves tuning in to someone else's emotions, self-empathy focuses inward, requiring you to understand and validate your own feelings. Self-empathy means nurturing your well-being, just as you'd care for others.

Self-empathy is far from selfish—it's about showing up for yourself. Ignoring your emotional needs leaves you depleted, much like a drought leaves the earth barren. By recognizing your needs and addressing them with compassion, you prevent the emotional drought that leaves you feeling drained and disconnected. Taking a moment to pause and show yourself kindness isn't about putting yourself above others—it's about sustaining your energy so that you can be there for the long haul. By doing so, you restore balance within yourself and create a ripple effect of well-being that benefits not only you but also those around you. Instead of running on empty, you replenish your inner resources, allowing yourself to be more patient, calm, and fully present in your life. Showing up for yourself is the foundation that allows you to show up for others.

Self-empathy can feel especially difficult when you're grappling with depression, anxiety, or past trauma. Depression often brings a sense of emotional numbness, disconnecting you from your own feelings, making them harder to recognize, let alone validate. With anxiety, emotions can feel overwhelming, preventing you from pausing long enough to consider your needs with compassion. Low self-worth, a common thread in both depression and anxiety, compounds the problem. If you believe you're undeserving of kindness, self-empathy feels out of reach.

Intense negative feelings such as these erode your sense of agency. This loss of agency, the feeling that you lack control or the ability to make meaningful choices, often fuels the cycle of negative self-talk and self-criticism that underlies depression and anxiety. Instead of extending compassion to yourself, you might fall into patterns of blaming yourself for your feelings, labeling yourself as weak or inadequate, which makes self-empathy feel like an impossible task.

When you're caught in this cycle, cognitive distortions—like catastrophizing or black-and-white thinking—magnify your flaws and struggles, making it hard to acknowledge the complexity of your emotional experience.

There's also a deep fear of vulnerability involved in practicing self-empathy. Facing and embracing your emotions—especially when they are raw and painful—can seem terrifying. You may worry that facing your feelings will only make them worse. Add to this the endless cycle of rumination, where your mind spins in circles, focusing on your pain and problems, making it difficult to shift from self-criticism to self-compassion.

"For Me" Statements and Self-Empathy

When intense emotions—whether joy, excitement, or more difficult feelings like anxiety and sadness—surface, it's easy to become overwhelmed or rush past them. Whether you're managing a storm of difficult emotions or savoring moments of happiness, amygdala whispering helps you stay grounded by offering linguistic empathy through two simple words: "for me."

"For me" statements create a gentle pause in your self-talk, turning it into a more compassionate and accepting dialogue. These words allow you to fully experience and affirm what you're feeling, whether you're struggling with pain or celebrating something positive. By using "for me," you offer yourself a gift of empathy. When you say, "This is *exhausting for me*," you're not just naming the emotion—you're also acknowledging its weight and offering yourself the gift of acceptance. You move from merely recognizing your emotions to accepting and affirming them. Those two words, "for me," help you honor and embrace your feelings with empathy and kindness.

Naming emotions not only lessens emotional intensity but also moves you from a reactive, fight-flight-or-freeze state to a more reflective, solution-focused mindset. Research by Lieberman et al. (2007) demonstrates that affect labeling reduces emotional intensity and enhances self-awareness, helping you transition from survival mode to intentional action. Recognizing and naming your emotions takes deliberate effort, especially when dealing with depression or anxiety, which often remains invisible to others. This invisibility makes external validation scarce, heightening the importance of self-compassion. Naming and affirming your feelings is essential for climbing upstairs to emotional clarity.

Below are named negative emotions paired with "for me" statements that demonstrate the language of self-empathy and provide context to each feeling. These examples are designed to help you integrate self-compassion into your own self-talk:

- It feels exhausting for me—when I'm drained from juggling too many responsibilities
- It feels overwhelming for me—when the weight of tasks and expectations crushes me

- It feels hopeless for me—when it seems like there's no way out of the situation
- It feels suffocating for me—when everything is too much, and I can't catch a breath
- It feels unbearable for me—when the emotional weight feels impossible to carry
- It feels like failure for me—when I feel like I'm falling short in every area of life
- It feels isolating for me—when I'm alone in my struggle, as if no one understands
- It feels disappointing for me—when I don't meet my own expectations
- It feels never-ending for me—when the challenges keep piling up without relief
- It feels discouraging for me—when no matter how hard I try, things don't improve

The examples below pair uplifting emotions with "for me" statements that help you savor and celebrate your positive experiences:

- It feels joyful for me—when I experience lightness, like everything is falling into place
- It feels fulfilling for me—when I'm deeply satisfied with what I'm doing
- It feels exciting for me—when new possibilities and opportunities are ahead
- It feels peaceful for me—when calmness surrounds me and nothing disturbs my peace
- It feels empowering for me—when I know I'm in control of my choices and future
- It feels uplifting for me—when optimism and energy lift my spirits
- It feels inspiring for me—when motivation pushes me toward new goals
- It feels reassuring for me—when I'm safe, supported, and understood
- It feels comforting for me—when I find warmth and solace in people or routines

Use these "for me" statements to help you with the next exercise on self-compassion.

"For Me" Statements: The Language of Self-Empathy

Recognize and name your emotional state. Begin by asking yourself, *Where is my mindset right now?* Are you in the basement of survival mode, caught in reactive thinking? Or are you upstairs, engaging in calm, reflective thought? Notice the direction you're heading—are you gradually moving toward clarity, or being pulled deeper into emotional overwhelm? Simply observing where you are, without judgment, is the first step toward offering yourself empathy. This awareness sets the stage for self-compassion, allowing you to understand your current state and respond with care.

Name your feelings, physical sensations, and thoughts. This step is about refining your language to articulate your emotions, physical sensations, and thoughts with precision. The more clearly you describe your experience, the easier it becomes to understand and manage your feelings. Naming your emotions transforms chaos into something tangible, giving you greater linguistic agency over how you process and respond.

Feelings (Emotional State)

Positive (Upstairs): ______________________________

Negative (Downstairs): ______________________________

Physical Sensations

Positive (Upstairs—e.g., "My shoulders feel relaxed, and my breathing is deep and steady"):

____

____

Negative (Downstairs—e.g., "There's tightness in my chest, my stomach is knotted, and my breathing is shallow"):

____

____

Self-Talk (Thoughts)

Positive (Upstairs—e.g., "I can handle this one step at a time"):

____

____

Negative (Downstairs—e.g., "I can't do this—everything is going wrong"):

____

____

Affirm and validate your emotions with "for me." Now, take your emotions, physical sensations, and thoughts and turn them into "for me" statements. Notice how this small change feels. What difference does it make for you? Does it bring more clarity, empathy, or understanding? Here are some examples to guide you:

Feelings (Emotional State)

I feel overwhelmed by all my responsibilities →

It feels overwhelming for me to manage so many responsibilities

____

____

Physical Sensations

My chest feels tight, and I'm finding it hard to breathe →

It feels constricting for me when my chest tightens, making each breath feel heavy

____

____

Self-Talk (Thoughts)

I'll never be able to get through this →

It feels crushing for me to think I'll never be able to get through this

____

____

Reflect on the following (in your head) as you apply this shift to your own responses:

- Was this process more challenging or easier than you expected?
- Did it feel helpful to personalize your experience in this way?
- What did you notice when you added "for me" to your responses?

This simple change in language creates space for self-compassion and understanding. By adding "for me," you offer yourself a chance to acknowledge and affirm your experience with kindness, which can help you see your emotions and thoughts in a more compassionate light.

"For You" Statements: A Path to Empathy and Connection

Just as "for me" statements cultivate self-empathy, "for you" statements are an equally powerful tool for extending empathy to others. These two simple words—"for you"—acknowledge the weight and intensity of another's emotions, especially when they may be operating in survival mode. By recognizing their struggle and naming how difficult their experience must be, you help create a space for them to feel understood and supported. For example, saying "It must feel overwhelming for you to juggle so many responsibilities" or "It must be exhausting for you to manage everything on your own" shifts the conversation from simple observation to one of shared understanding. This validates their experience without minimizing its impact, offering empathy that feels genuine and supportive.

"For you" statements aren't limited to challenging emotions; they can also be used to celebrate positive and uplifting moments. For instance, "It must feel incredibly rewarding for you to see your hard work paying off" or "It must be exciting for you to embrace this new opportunity" allows you to acknowledge and celebrate their achievements, reinforcing the joy they feel and making the moment more meaningful.

By incorporating both "for you" and "for me" statements, especially in the context of intense emotions and situations, you infuse your language with empathy, making it a practical tool for staying grounded. These statements help you and others shift from the reactive, fight-flight-or-freeze response in the basement to the more reflective, thoughtful space of the upstairs brain, where critical thinking occurs. Here, far more choices are available—choices that allow for problem-solving, connection, and growth beyond the limitations of survival mode.

"For You" Statements: The Language of Empathy for Others

In this exercise, you'll learn how to use "for you" statements to offer empathy and deepen your relationships with *others*. By tuning in to emotional and physical cues, you can discern when someone is stuck in survival mode (downstairs) and offer the support they need to feel understood. These subtle but profound shifts in language can transform conversations, moving them from reactive to reflective and fostering deeper emotional connections.

Discern their emotional and physical state (upstairs and downstairs). Think back to a recent intense situation where someone close to you was reactive or short-tempered. A clipped or abrasive tone, visible irritability, rushed or abrupt movements, or becoming withdrawn and uncommunicative often indicates that someone is "downstairs." In contrast, those operating upstairs tend to present with a composed demeanor, marked by measured responses and steady physical presence. By discerning these behavioral patterns, you gain deeper insight into their emotional landscape, enabling you to respond with more thoughtful and empathetic engagement.

Weave "for you" statements into their emotions and actions. Once you've identified their emotions and actions, use "for you" statements to reflect empathy and validate their feelings. Your goal is to convey that you see and acknowledge what they are going through. For instance, if someone appears angry or overwhelmed, you might say, "It must feel overwhelming for you to juggle everything when you're already feeling stretched thin."

Observe their response. If they nod or affirm your statement, you've created a meaningful connection. If they clarify or adjust the emotion—perhaps indicating they're more annoyed than overwhelmed—acknowledge the shift and reflect it back: "That must be incredibly annoying for you."

Observe the shift. As you practice using "for you" statements in conversations, pay attention to emotional shifts. Are they still stuck in the basement (reactive) or transitioning upstairs (calmer and more reflective)? Did your "for you" statement help them feel understood or less defensive? Did they help transition the person from survival mode to a more reflective state? Consider how this practice enhanced the emotional tone of your interactions and your ability to connect more deeply with others.

Embracing Positive Moments

Besides self-empathy, another powerful tool in the solution-focused toolkit is embracing positive moments. Problems aren't constant; their frequency and intensity can vary. By identifying moments when problems are less frequent or absent, you can focus on times when those issues did not exist (de Shazer 1988).

Life is a series of moments, and engaging in the habit of recognizing, remembering, and replicating individual, small, positive moments can establish a pattern of self-care and improve your well-being. Reflecting on these positive differences helps you transform your thoughts, actions, and behaviors. When you recognize which actions bring you joy and peace, you can repeat and build upon these positive experiences. These micro-moments, already woven into the fabric of your life, hold the power to rekindle hope. Their significance lies in their deeply personal nature, making them easier to recognize and replicate, as they are uniquely yours.

Take the example of overworked educators who reconnected with their joy in teaching by focusing on small positive moments elsewhere in their lives.

Overworked Teachers Discovering Positive Differences

A group of overworked teachers faced intense fatigue, anxiety, and depression. They dealt with the stress of school shootings, political tensions, endless meetings, continuous mandates, higher emotional needs of children, COVID-19–related learning delays, and a lack of appreciation. This stress manifested at home, where they struggled to separate work from personal life. They spent evenings grading papers and answered email late into the night. To help them cope, they were asked to reflect on the following questions:

When did you feel less stressed and more motivated to work, even for a short time?

What kept you going despite the stress?

What small positive moments in your day brought you joy?

How did you foster these small brighter moments?

What do you know about yourself that can help you continue nurturing these positive moments?

On a scale of 1–10, where 10 is very confident and 1 is the opposite, how confident are you that you can incorporate more of these positive differences into your life? What keeps your number from being lower?

What gives you confidence that you'll engage in at least one small activity that brings you joy?

Through reflection, the teachers began to uncover simple yet impactful activities unique to each of them. One teacher, feeling the weight of their anxiety, decided to commit to a Zoom Pilates class for physical and mental relief, helping her regain balance in life. Another teacher found solace in creative expression. Writing a funny poem for a friend lightened her mood and brought a sense of joy and accomplishment to her day. Another found that participating in community activities provided a sense of belonging and emotional nourishment.

By focusing on their unique positive differences, they discovered personalized ways to bring joy into their lives. These actions enabled them to nurture and sustain themselves, opening up new perspectives and motivating them to continue.

Now, it's your opportunity to embrace positive micro-moments.

Nurturing Positive Differences in the Present

In today's fast-moving world, it's easy to get swept up in the rush and overlook the present. This constant motion can prevent you from noticing the small yet meaningful moments that bring joy and fulfillment. By slowing down to reflect and appreciate these *sparks of delight*—those subtle but powerful moments—you can enrich your well-being. This exercise encourages you to reflect on the *peaks of your week* and explore how to nurture more of those positive experiences.

Recall a recent instance this past week that brought you a sense of joy or peace. Reflect on how you navigated moments of anxiety, found small pockets of tranquility, or took care of your own needs. How did these moments enrich your life, and how might you welcome more of them into your everyday experience?

What positive experiences have you noticed in the past week that you want to keep happening? Take a moment to reflect on the *peaks of your week*—those moments that brought a spark of joy or fulfillment. What stood out to you, and how did it lift your spirits?

____

____

____

____

____

____

____

____

Have you always been aware of these positive moments, or is this new for you? Consider how these positive differences—these *sparks of delight*—feel compared to past experiences. Are they new, or have they always been there but gone unnoticed? Reflect on how these *peaks of your week* have shaped your recent days. What allowed you to notice them now, and how might you continue to invite more of these moments into your life moving forward?

____

____

____

____

Were these moments helpful for you? Take a moment to reflect on their influence. How have these *peaks of your week* contributed to your overall well-being? In what ways have they enriched your life, and how might they have positively impacted others around you?

____

____

____

____

How did you bring these moments into being? Consider the actions you took that allowed these *sparks of delight* to unfold. What choices or efforts led to these moments of joy or fulfillment?

____

____

____

____

There may be times when the actions that once brought you joy are no longer possible. Perhaps you can no longer take long walks or spend time with a close friend. In these moments, reflect on how you've adapted. What strategies did you use to cope with these changes? How did you pivot, even in small ways, to create new moments of peace or joy? Reflect on how you've embraced these changes with compassion and acceptance.

___

___

___

___

Taking time to reflect on these moments reinforces the positive actions you've taken and reminds you of what is working. The power to create more of these moments lies within you, and by continuing to nurture what has worked, you can shape a future that is brighter and more fulfilling.

Using Compliments to Empower Yourself

Compliments are powerful, solution-focused tools that can empower you by highlighting the strengths and resources already present in your life. As you reflect on the positive differences you've noticed in your life—the *sparks of delight* and *peaks of your week*—consider how these moments connect to compliments. When you recognize these positive moments, you're acknowledging qualities in yourself that made them possible. Compliments are an extension of this recognition, a way to honor those qualities with appreciation.

Appreciation means seeing and valuing the qualities that make a difference, both in yourself and in others. When you take the time to observe and appreciate, you're acknowledging what is good, meaningful, and effective. Appreciation, in the form of compliments, is a way of honoring these strengths. It reinforces positive behaviors and affirms the impact they have, both on yourself and those around you. In this way, compliments become more than words—they become tools for building confidence, nurturing self-worth, and fostering connection. By recognizing what you appreciate, you empower yourself and others to keep growing and contributing to a brighter, more fulfilling life.

What do you most appreciate about yourself? What qualities or actions have you noticed that bring value to your life? And when you look at others, what do you appreciate about them?

Direct Compliments

In the solution-focused approach, there are two types of compliments: direct and indirect. Direct compliments are an explicit expression of praise, appreciation, or admiration. Most likely, you're fluent in the direct compliment. Direct compliments may include commending others on their coping abilities, congratulating their achievements, acknowledging their skills at work, or admiring their perseverance, passion, honesty, and determination. Examples include: "I'm impressed with how you reached out for help instead of isolating yourself at home" or "It's impressive how you managed to cope with your immense challenges while still caring for your loved ones."

Indirect Compliments and Coping Questions

Indirect compliments are in the form of the following question: "How did I do it?" Notice the question is not "Did I do it?" Rather, it's "*How* did I do it?" The word "how" communicates "in what manner and by what means." The helping verb "did" (past tense) conveys that you have done it before and thus can do it again. The main verb "to do" (accomplish, perform, manage, endure, stop, think, decide, choose) highlights the actions you have already taken to achieve your goals.

Indirect compliments are gifts in the form of a question, and they can be given to yourself and to others. Offering yourself compliments may feel indulgent at first, but it is actually a powerful way to activate self-compassion and recognize your own achievements. Much like using "for me" statements, this practice is about self-care and fostering self-awareness.

Unlike direct compliments, which can often be dismissed or downplayed, indirect compliments—especially when framed as a question—tend to feel more natural and easier to accept. This subtle approach invites reflection and self-recognition, making it more likely that the compliment will resonate. As a result, indirect compliments become a powerful tool for fostering personal growth and strengthening relationships, gently encouraging both yourself and others to acknowledge and appreciate the actions that lead to positive change.

Notice the examples below, where difficult situations are first acknowledged with "for me" statements, followed by direct and indirect compliments.

Observation	"For Me" Statement	Direct Self-Compliment	Indirect Self-Compliment in Question Form
A woman struggling with depression was barely able to get out of bed and help her children get to school.	It feels exhausting *for me* to care for my children while fighting through the fog of my depression.	I'm proud of how I've managed to get my children to school, despite feeling so exhausted.	**How** did I *manage* to get them to school on time given how I have been feeling?
A father acknowledged he was feeling depressed and had little patience dealing with his sixteen-year-old son, who lied about using alcohol with his friends. He tried to stay calm, but sometimes he became angry and irritable, worsening his own feelings of depression.	It feels so scary *for me* to worry about my son's safety, especially knowing he's been lying about using alcohol. It's disappointing *for me* to find out he hasn't been honest with me, and it's frustrating *for me* that this has worsened my own feelings of depression.	I appreciate how hard I've been trying to protect him and talk to him about his substance use, even while managing my depression.	**How** have I *managed* to stay calm, even if only at times? How have I dealt with my depression while still doing my best to keep him safe?
A woman who recently became sober was working hard on her recovery and began experiencing intense cravings to drink. She started to plan how she would get her next drink.	These cravings feel so intense *for me*, and even though I know it's normal, it's still really intense *for me* to handle.	I appreciate my honesty in acknowledging my cravings and recognizing that I've even started to plan how I would get my next drink. It takes a lot of courage to face these feelings so openly.	**How** have I *coped* with these cravings? **How** did I *make the decision* to acknowledge my cravings instead of hiding them? **How** have I been able *to sustain* my recovery through these intense experiences?

These examples illustrate how subtle language changes can transform how you give and receive compliments. By thoughtfully adjusting your language, you can offer indirect compliments that uplift both yourself and others, creating space for appreciation and deeper connection. When offering self-compliments, ask "How did I do it?"—a question that activates your agency, much like "for me" statements nurture self-empathy. Similarly, when complimenting others, ask "How did you do it?" to recognize their efforts while offering "for you" statements to show others empathy.

These subtle adjustments not only reinforce personal agency but also cultivate healthier, more meaningful interactions. Such shifts in language require practice and intention to truly take root. Mastering indirect compliments takes practice, but it helps build fluency in solution-focused language. Today, take a moment to practice—whether at home, at work, with your children, or even in a brief encounter. Offer both "for me" and "for you" statements, and ask "How did I do it?" and "How did you do it?" Notice how these small shifts in language lead to more meaningful interactions, spreading hope and empathy to both yourself and those around you.

While simple in structure, these linguistic changes are powerful tools for expressing empathy and fostering hope, empowering both you and others through careful phrasing and thoughtful sentence construction.

Shifting from Problem-Focused to Solution-Focused Self-Talk

When you're in an amygdala storm—caught in the emotional intensity of the basement—shifting to solution-focused language is especially hard. In these moments, your brain is in survival mode, reinforcing negative self-talk and amplifying feelings of helplessness. Yet, with intentional practice, you can start to pull yourself out of this reactive state and engage in more constructive self-dialogue.

Most of us instinctively zero in on problems, especially when anxiety or stress kicks in. This tendency is only magnified when you're managing depression or anxiety. Problem-focused language becomes our "mother tongue," making it difficult to see potential solutions. The first step is simply recognizing this habit, which allows you to begin shifting toward more empowering, solution-oriented language.

The distinction between a self-monologue and a self-dialogue is key here. A monologue traps you in one-sided, often problem-focused thinking, whereas a dialogue invites reflection and questions. By asking yourself, *What small step can I take right now?* or *How have I managed tough situations before?* you open the door to a conversation with yourself that is both constructive and compassionate. This transformation takes patience, especially during an amygdala storm, but the shift from complaint to solution is within your reach.

Learning a new self-dialogue can be an empowering and rewarding process. Just like learning any language, fluency builds with consistent practice, even if it's just a few minutes each day. Though it may feel challenging at first, each step you take nurtures growth. With gentle persistence, you begin to see meaningful progress. Over time, these small efforts help you develop a personalized, solution-focused inner dialogue that strengthens resilience, fosters self-compassion, and opens new possibilities for how you relate to yourself.

Transforming Complaints into Solutions

Who hasn't indulged in a satisfying complaint? Complaining can bring temporary relief, offering connection, validation, or support from others. It's a shared human experience. However, when you consistently rely on problem-focused language—especially in your inner dialogue—negative self-talk shapes how you see yourself. It starts to dominate your inner dialogue. Instead of asking constructive questions like *What did I do well today?* or *How can I handle this differently next time?* you may automatically think, *Why does everything go wrong?* or *Why am I so bad at this?* Without realizing it, you rely on negative and passive words that reinforce feelings of helplessness.

By gradually shifting your internal language from complaints to questions, you create space for self-compassion. You have the power to transform how you speak to yourself, but this shift—from problem-focused to solution-focused language—requires careful attention to the exact words you use. It's especially challenging when your mind races and you slip into the rapid-fire rhythm of your "mother tongue"—problem talk. How do you pause? How do you take a moment?

As you've been learning throughout this chapter, it starts by affirming your experience with "for me." Let's look at an example to illustrate how this practice unfolds.

Consider a mother at the end of a chaotic day. She sighs, feeling defeated, and mutters, "I'm failing at everything—there's just too much to do, and I never get it right." Her words are weighed down with self-criticism and doubt. She repeats phrases like "I can't keep up" and "Nothing I do makes a difference," each thought deepening her sense of failure. Every task feels endless, her efforts lost under the weight of unattainable expectations, and she spirals further into exhaustion.

Within her complaints, subtle clues to her resilience are hidden in her language. Paying close attention to the *exact words* she uses during moments of frustration reveals the strengths already present, even when clouded by self-doubt:

- "There's too much to do"—This highlights that she is actively *doing* a lot, showing her commitment to her responsibilities and her continued effort.
- "I never get it right"—This suggests she is *striving to get things right*, indicating her desire for improvement and care about the outcomes.
- "I can't keep up"—The fact that she feels she can't keep up implies that she has been doing her best to manage everything.
- "Nothing I do makes a difference"—The word "do" underscores that she is consistently *taking action*. Her desire to *make a difference* points to her dedication, even if she feels like her efforts are going unnoticed.

Despite her feelings of defeat, these phrases show that she is *actively engaged*, *working hard*, and *trying to make a difference*—all reflections of her perseverance and deep care.

To take this further, you can turn these positive words into solution-focused questions that invite self-reflection and growth. For example:

- *What have I been able to do, even when it feels overwhelming?*
- *How have I kept going, despite feeling like I never get it right?*
- *Who has noticed the difference I've been trying to make?*
- *When do I feel like my actions make the biggest impact?*
- *Where have I already succeeded in small ways that I haven't yet recognized?*

By focusing on these questions, you shift from self-criticism to self-discovery. Listening closely to your own words helps you uncover the hidden strengths and solutions that have been there all along.

Learning to speak to yourself in this new way is much like learning a new language. Just as mastering a second language requires motivation, practice, and an understanding of sentence structure, learning to speak with self-compassion and agency also demands effort. The first step is motivation—the desire to shift from negative, passive self-talk to one that embraces solutions and actions. Then comes practice—building fluency in recognizing positive actions even amid struggles. And finally, it requires an understanding of how language shapes thought. The words and verbs we choose can either trap us in defeat or propel us toward growth.

By practicing this new "language," you train yourself to listen for solutions embedded in complaints, both in your inner dialogue and in your conversations with others. This shift—from focusing on what's wrong to recognizing what's already working—breaks the cycle of negativity and transforms moments of frustration into opportunities for growth. The strengths have been there all along; it's just a matter of noticing them.

Coping Questions

One particularly effective tool for uncovering these hidden strengths is the use of coping questions. Indirect compliments often function as coping questions—for example, "**How** did you *keep going*?" These open-ended questions appreciate the strength and resilience you've demonstrated in the face of adversity. By shifting the focus from victimhood or self-blame to one of quiet strength, coping questions can change your narrative.

Without purposeful self-reflection, it can be difficult to see your own coping abilities. Coping questions offer gentle guidance, helping you recognize the ways in which you've navigated tough moments, often without even realizing it. No matter how small these efforts may seem, they are the building blocks for moving forward, one step at a time. Even the tiniest successes—whether it's holding yourself together during a tense meeting or simply managing to get out of bed—are worth celebrating.

Shifting Complaints to Solutions

This exercise will guide you through transforming complaints into actionable insights using solution-focused language. By following these steps, you'll learn to recognize your strengths and shift your mindset toward self-compassion, resilience, and growth.

Indulge in a complaint. Start by reflecting on a recent situation that left you feeling frustrated, irritated, or stressed. Maybe it was a conflict at work or a difficult conversation with a friend. Write down all your complaints without holding back. Example: Imagine you were frustrated by a conversation where you felt unheard—"They didn't even listen to me! It's not fair—I was trying my best, and they just kept interrupting me."

____

____

____

____

Create "for me" statements. Now, take your complaints and transform them with "for me" statements. This step helps you validate your feelings without judgment. By adding "for me," you're creating a compassionate dialogue with yourself, recognizing how personal and valid your feelings are. Example: In the earlier scenario, your statement might become these "for me" statements—"It feels frustrating for me when I try to explain myself and feel unheard" or "It feels exhausting for me to put in effort and not be acknowledged."

____

____

____

Find positive words in your complaint. Look through your complaints and "for me" statements to identify any positive or neutral words that reflect effort, persistence, or intention. Even in challenging situations, you were likely trying to accomplish something. Example: The earlier complaint mentioned "trying my best." This is a positive effort, showing care and engagement.

____

____

____

Ask yourself appreciative questions. Reflect on what you most appreciate about yourself in this situation, even amid the frustration. Ask yourself, *What do I most appreciate about how I handled this situation? What else?* Example: "I appreciate how I kept calm, even when I felt ignored." "I recognize that I tried my best to express myself clearly despite the interruptions."

____

____

____

Ask yourself solution-focused questions. These questions highlight possible paths forward and help you reflect on what you learned from the situation. These questions will activate your solution-focused mindset. Example: "What helped me stay composed when I felt frustrated?" "How did I continue to try and express myself?"

____

____

____

By practicing these steps regularly, you'll start to recognize strengths within your complaints, turning frustration into opportunities for growth. These simple shifts allow you to replace negative self-talk with compassionate, solution-focused language, helping you manage challenges more effectively.

Too Much Cream Cheese

Monika, an exhausted medical resident, had just finished a grueling night on call, dealing with nonstop emergencies. When asked in session to complain about something—anything—she found even this simple task challenging in her fatigued state. She sighed and muttered, "They put too much cream cheese on my bagel."

What seemed like a trivial complaint held deeper meaning for Monika. She paused and reflected, "It feels frustrating for me because I was really looking forward to one peaceful moment in my chaotic day." She realized that her bagel, simple as it was, symbolized a brief moment of self-care amid the chaos.

Then she asked herself, "What do I appreciate about myself in this moment?" She thought for a moment and acknowledged, "I appreciate that, even though I'm beyond tired, I still made a point to do something kind for myself." This small act of treating herself to a bagel wasn't just a snack—it was a deliberate choice to carve out a moment of care in a relentless schedule.

Next, Monika asked herself, "How did I manage to find time for this small moment of joy, even when everything feels overwhelming?" She realized she had intentionally made space for it. "I made the choice to prioritize myself, even if just for a few minutes, because I know it helps me recharge," she said.

With this reflection, she uncovered a solution. Monika discovered that *choosing* small, intentional moments of self-care gave her the energy she needed to face the rest of her demanding day. This awareness turned what initially felt like an insignificant frustration into a valuable strategy for navigating her high-pressure environment.

Then she asked, "How helpful has it been for me to make time for these small acts of kindness?" She rated it an 8 out of 10.

Finally, she asked, "How confident am I that I can do at least one kind thing for myself each day?" Monika smiled and rated it a 9 out of 10, realizing that even amid the chaos, moments of care were not only possible—they were within her control.

By asking herself solution-focused questions, Monika uncovered practical solutions for managing her stress and felt her narrative shift. What began as a simple complaint had transformed into a deeper recognition of her ability to care for herself: "I managed to sneak in some self-care, and even found a way to laugh about it."

Navigating Breaking Points

Sometimes, life hands you moments so intense, it feels impossible to survive the next five or ten minutes, let alone an entire day. In those breaking point moments, when the weight of reality presses down so hard that it's difficult to breathe, focusing on smaller, more manageable increments of time can help you regain a sense of control. Breaking your coping into ten-minute intervals can make the unbearable feel tolerable. Whether five, ten, or thirty minutes, the goal is to focus on what feels achievable.

Coping Ten Minutes at a Time

Reflect on a breaking-point moment. Reflect on a moment that felt particularly overwhelming or hard to manage. For instance, Ben, a college student during finals week, learned that his mother had been diagnosed with breast cancer. Already under pressure to maintain his grades or lose financial aid, Ben was also dealing with a close friend who had dropped out and was struggling with substance abuse. On top of it all, Ben had just fought with his partner. Everything felt too heavy to handle.

Write down your experience, vividly describing the emotions, physical sensations, and thoughts that ran through your mind. Capture what it felt like in the moment. Example: *It all crashed down at once. My mom's diagnosis felt like a punch in the gut, but I had finals and couldn't stop to process it. My fight with my partner left me feeling completely isolated. My heart raced, my hands trembled, and I couldn't stop thinking,* I can't handle this; everything is falling apart. *I didn't know where to turn.*

____

____

____

____

____

____

Write two "for me" statements. Name the emotions you experienced and add "for me" at the end. This brings empathy into your reflection, connecting you to your emotions with compassion. Example: *It feels devastating for me to know my mom is battling cancer while I'm stuck here, wanting to help. It feels overwhelming for me to juggle finals, financial stress, and fear for my friend's well-being.*

____

____

____

____

____

What do you most appreciate about yourself? Reflect on what you most appreciate about how you navigated the moment, even when it felt unbearable. Think about your strength, courage, or persistence. Example: *I appreciate that, despite everything, I continued studying, even when it was difficult to focus. I also reached out to my partner, acknowledging how my stress had affected them. I offered a sincere apology and made a plan for us to spend quality time together, creating space for connection and healing.*

____

____

____

____

____

Assess how well you handled it. On a scale of 1–10, rate how well you managed the situation, with 10 being you handled it the best way you could and 1 meaning the opposite. Example: *I'd give myself a 5.*

____

What kept your number from being lower? Identify the strengths or strategies that helped prevent your rating from being lower. This helps you acknowledge what worked, even in small ways. Example: *I called my mom and we both appreciated the conversation. I plowed through and finished finals. I let my partner know what stress I was experiencing and apologized for my irritable behavior.*

____

____

____

____

Is your number good enough? What would you be doing at your good enough number? If the number feels good enough, reflect on what worked. If not, think about what you could do next time to raise your score by one point. Example: *A 7 would be good enough. I'd take more time to pause, appreciate how difficult this is for me, and reach out for help sooner. I'd also schedule more self-care breaks in my day.*

____

____

____

What can you do for yourself in the next ten minutes? Consider one thing you can do right now to increase your number. Example: *I can pause, write down what I appreciate about myself, and take a short walk.*

____

____

Whether it's focusing on the next ten minutes or another short time frame, this practice encourages you to recognize your strengths and use self-compassion during breaking point moments. By focusing on what you can do in the present, you can break overwhelming moments into manageable chunks.

Asserting Your Needs

Wants are different from needs. Needs are essential human requirements necessary for survival. When you're experiencing uncomfortable feelings such as anger, sadness, frustration, hopelessness, annoyance, anxiety, fear, panic, or worry, this strongly signals that you have needs that aren't being met. Asking yourself, *What do I need right now?* is a compassionate question that recognizes and affirms that you do have needs and helps you develop a plan for how to meet them.

Understanding and meeting your needs is a fundamental aspect of holistic well-being. While needs vary from person to person, they generally include physical comfort, safety, meaningful relationships, and a sense of self-worth.

Scaling Your Needs Right Now

Scaling your needs creates a gradual path for growth, much like building a staircase or gently ascending a hill. Taking one small step at a time allows you to address your needs in manageable increments and be kind to yourself. There's no instant way out of the depression and anxiety basement; each step builds on the previous one, and your journey will be unique to you.

Reflect on a recent stressful situation you experienced and consider the following questions. On a scale from 1–10, where 10 is the best and 1 is the opposite:

How well did you recognize and affirm that your needs are valid and essential?

____

How well did you assert what you needed to yourself and others?

____

Now, for each of the above questions, ask yourself the following questions:

What kept your number from being lower?

____

____

____

What would be a good enough number? If your number is good enough, what do you want to keep doing that is working for you? If your number isn't good enough, what is one thing you could do to increase your number?

____

____

____

Who would notice you advocating for your needs? What number would they give you regarding how well you have advocated for your needs from 1–10? What accounts for the similarities or differences in your number?

____

____

____

____

As you can see from this exercise, addressing your needs is a multifaceted process. Navigating your needs requires ongoing practice and remaining attuned to yourself. By engaging in these solution-focused actions, you create practical steps to navigate your challenges with self-compassion.

Carl and Elizabeth's Family Braves a Storm

Remember Elizabeth and Carl from chapter 2? Carl was dealing with multiple sclerosis, and the whole family faced challenges in learning to support Carl and adjust their own lives. This story illustrates how they navigated a storm together by observing their distress and recognizing their needs.

One morning, Carl suddenly lost the ability to walk. Elizabeth, feeling overwhelmed, couldn't manage alone. The thought of Carl being paralyzed plunged her into overwhelming fear and sorrow. Carl was gripped by panic, unable to move or even make it to the bathroom. Fearing reliance on a wheelchair, his mind raced with uncertainties. To compound matters, they were in the middle of a snowstorm, with the hospital an hour away.

Mark, visiting with his pregnant wife, was abruptly awakened by his mother's frantic plea to rush Carl to the emergency room. As Mark processed the news, a mixture of shock and sadness overcame him. He cherished memories of his father's playful spirit from his own childhood and hoped his own child would grow up with similar joyful moments shared with Carl. However, with his father's worsening condition, that hopeful future now seemed uncertain.

Amid the chaos, Elizabeth and Carl focused on the present moment, taking deep breaths and breaking down tasks into manageable steps.

They agreed it was worth the drive to take Carl to the hospital where he receives his care, even though it meant a longer drive. Carl remained composed in the wheelchair, sipping water while Elizabeth and Mark prepared their belongings. Mark navigated the snowstorm, drawing upon his experience as an EMT who had driven in worse blizzard conditions. Jazz music soothed their frayed nerves as they concentrated on reaching the hospital safely.

Here is how Carl and Elizabeth applied some of the tools from this chapter:

What "for you" statements could Elizabeth and Mark give to each other?

Elizabeth to Carl: "Managing this sudden change must be *scary for you.*"

Mark to Elizabeth: "Seeing Dad like this must be *terrifying for you.*"

Elizabeth to Mark: "This must be *intense for you* to see your father in this condition while waiting for the birth of your first child."

What "for me" statements could they give themselves?

Elizabeth: "It's *overwhelming for me*, and I need reassurance that we're all in this together."

Carl: "This loss of mobility is *scary for me*, and I need to know that I can still contribute in my own way."

Mark: "Seeing my father like this is *really sad for me*, and I need support to stay strong for him."

What direct and indirect compliments could they give one another?

Elizabeth to Mark: "You're doing a great job navigating through this snowstorm. **How** are you *staying so calm?*

Carl to Elizabeth: "You're always so strong for us. Thank you. **How** do you *stay* so strong?"

Mark to Elizabeth: "**How** do you *stay* so calm and organized despite everything you're juggling?"

Elizabeth to Carl: "**How** do you *manage* to stay composed and sip water even though you were in such distress? **How** were you *able* to stay calm while I got your needed belongings for the hospital?"

Elizabeth, Carl, and Mark exhibited remarkable strength and resourcefulness in the face of adversity. Though undoubtedly stressed, they dealt with it by acknowledging their emotions, thinking through their options, and relying on their past experiences. Their renewed narrative shifted from panic and helplessness to resilience and teamwork.

Bringing Amygdala Whispering Skills Together

You've been learning how to calm your amygdala storms with grace and compassion, and now it's time to put all those skills into practice. This exercise helps you reflect on a recent stressful situation, affirm your progress, and take active steps toward addressing your needs in the moment.

Reflect on a recent stressful situation. Think about a moment when you felt stuck in the basement of your brain—where stress or emotional overwhelm took over. Write three "for me" statements, affirming your emotions in a compassionate way.

____

____

____

____

Identify how you coped and what you need. How did you cope with the situation? Reflect on any steps, big or small, that helped you move through it. What do you need? What would help you right now?

____

____

____

____

Direct compliments. Give yourself three direct compliments about how you handled the situation. Notice the words you used and pick out the positive language within your experience.

____

____

____

____

Indirect compliments. Now, ask yourself solution-focused questions customized from the positive words you discovered in your description. Start questions with what, how, who, when, and where.

____

____

____

____

Rate how well you coped. On a scale from 1–10, rate how well you think you managed the situation, where 10 is the best and 1 is the opposite?

____

What kept your number from being lower? Reflect on what you did that kept your number from being lower.

____

____

____

____

Making a plan. What is one thing you can do in the next ten minutes that would be helpful for you? On a scale of 1–10, how confident are you that you'll do your best to take one step toward addressing your needs in the next ten minutes? What gives you this confidence?

____

____

____

____

____

Through these steps, you're not just surviving stressful situations—you're learning how to recognize your strengths, respond to your needs, and move toward a solution-focused mindset with self-compassion. Each small step builds resilience and makes navigating future challenges more manageable.

Congratulations on completing chapter 3! You're well on your way to becoming a skilled amygdala whisperer. In the next chapter, you'll discover how to view your most important relationships as valuable resources for building solutions. By cultivating meaningful relationships using solution-focused strategies, you empower yourself to expand your coping possibilities, quickly shift your perspective, and envision a hopeful future.

CHAPTER 4

Recognizing Valuable Relationships: Nurturing Your Support Network

In the previous chapter, you explored the inner strengths that have anchored you through life's emotional storms—guiding you as you climbed from the basement of survival to the upstairs of clarity and growth. You applied early lessons from chapters 1 and 2, such as finding moments of delight and noticing your actions during distress and resilience. You also learned to calm your brain's emergency response, allowing your prefrontal cortex to engage—where you can think clearly, reason, and explore new possibilities.

As you recognize how you've been climbing out of the basement—where you sought refuge during emotional storms—and into the upstairs of your life, where clarity and growth reside, envision your transformation. Picture new roots anchoring you, steady even in the winds of a haboob, preventing you from being tossed like a tumbleweed. See fresh leaves unfurling, absorbing warmth and nourishment, while new branches stretch out toward support and new possibilities.

Very Important Presences: Expanding the Influences in Your Life

When you think of "VIPs"—Very Important People—you likely focus on people who bring positivity: family, friends, mentors—individuals who uplift and inspire you, who offer guidance and support. This chapter broadens and redefines VIPs to encompass Very Important Presences—influences that shape life in both obvious and subtle ways, whether nurturing or challenging.

Throughout this book, you've been tapping into your internal resources—strength, resilience, and self-awareness—to navigate life's complexities. Yet, your external resources, these presences, also play a crucial role in guiding your thoughts and decisions. Some quietly lift you up, offering support and helping you see new perspectives. Others may weigh you down, draining your energy or clouding your thinking. Regardless of how they show up, these presences shift and evolve over time, constantly influencing how you move through the world.

These VIPs extend beyond people and include any significant force that impacts your emotional landscape. This could be the quiet comfort of a pet, the demands of a chronic illness, or even fleeting interactions that leave an imprint on your day. Presence extends far beyond physical proximity; it is the emotional and mental influence that leaves a lasting imprint on your thoughts, actions, and decisions. It might be the guidance of a mentor, the memory of a loved one, the daily challenge of managing a health condition, or the spiritual energy that brings you peace. Whether these presences support your growth or test your resilience, they shape the choices you make and the direction you take.

Throughout this chapter, you'll explore how these presences—whether drawn from people, experiences, or environments—affect your choices and internal world. Some presences may energize and uplift, while others test your endurance or prompt reflection, pushing you to evolve. Each presence, whether prominent or subtle, plays a dynamic role in your journey.

VIPs in your life—whether people, memories, or experiences—are essential to your mental and emotional health. Strong connections provide a sense of belonging and reduce feelings of isolation, which can deeply impact your well-being. When you nurture meaningful relationships, you create opportunities to see new perspectives, shift rigid thoughts, and open the door to positive change. These connections offer support that helps you navigate life's challenges more easily.

Loneliness, however, can erode these important connections. It affects up to one-third of people in industrialized countries (Cacioppo and Cacioppo 2018) and is a significant factor in depression and anxiety. Studies show that loneliness not only increases mental health struggles but also contributes to physical health risks like heart disease and stroke (Cacioppo et al. 2015; Park et al. 2020). When you feel lonely, your body is signaling the need for reconnection—much like hunger signals the need for food.

If loneliness or social isolation is taking a toll on your health, solution-focused questions can guide you toward building or repairing those vital relationships. In a solution-focused approach, you engage with these presences intentionally, using them as resources. For example, ask yourself, *What would this person or presence encourage me to do next? How has this presence guided me before, and how can it guide me now? Who in my life brings me comfort, and how can I spend more time with them?* or *What small step can I take to reach out to someone today?* These questions help shift your focus from isolation to action, empowering you to reconnect with the VIPs who matter most.

Even in situations where social interaction is limited, you can still cultivate positive solitude—time spent alone intentionally, which can enhance emotional regulation and overall well-being (Weinstein et al. 2023). Reflecting with questions like *How can I use this time alone to recharge?* or *What activities bring me peace when I'm on my own?* allows you to see solitude as an opportunity for growth rather than isolation.

Ultimately, recognizing the role of your VIPs—both in relationships and within yourself—offers you a path out of loneliness and into deeper, more fulfilling connections. By regularly engaging with solution-focused questions, you take charge of your well-being and open up possibilities for healing and transformation.

Engaging with Presences Through Solution-Focused Questions

Building on the solution-focused questions introduced earlier, you'll now apply them to the broader range of VIPs in your life. These questions are designed to open new perspectives and possibilities, like throwing open windows to flood a dark room with light. Just as light reveals hidden details, these questions help you appreciate the terrain of your life, guiding you toward the next steps with clarity and purpose.

Below are examples of how you can reflect on the presences (influences) in your life—whether uplifting or challenging—and transform them into opportunities for growth. Each question illuminates the diverse paths before you, offering clarity and choices for how you navigate your unique terrain.

What did I do today that helped me manage my condition a little bit more easily?

What have I discovered about myself that has helped me stay resilient in the face of this presence?

What do I know has helped me embrace this presence as an opportunity for growth?

What can I focus on that brings me even a few minutes of relief or calm?

How have I adapted my routine to make living with this presence easier?

How have I been able to notice, pause, and embrace this presence in my life?

How have I limited the unhealthy impact of this presence in my daily life?

Who has provided me some comfort during this difficult time?

Who do I know would be helpful to reach out to that has dealt with similar challenges, and what can I learn from their experience?

Who might benefit from what I've learned, and how can I share my experience?

When have I noticed and taken a moment to appreciate the helpful presences in my life?

When have I observed presences and influences that have brought me joy?

When can I set aside time for self-care to counterbalance the weight of this presence?

Where have I been when I noticed this positive presence in my daily life?

Where have I been when I took a moment to appreciate the presences in my life?

Where do I know there are resources or tools to help me manage this presence more effectively?

Navigating Complex Presences Through Reflection

Complex presences refer to relationships or external influences that introduce emotional, mental, or psychological strain into daily life. These might involve challenging connections with family members, friends, or colleagues or external pressures like chronic illness, financial stress, societal issues, or political tensions. Though these presences may feel overwhelming or beyond your control, they simultaneously open doors to growth, reflection, and resilience.

By incorporating solution-focused coping questions, you can reclaim a sense of agency when these influences seem beyond your reach. These questions guide you toward actionable steps and positive shifts, empowering you to navigate these intricate dynamics with greater clarity and intention.

For example, when dealing with a chronic illness, asking yourself, *What small steps have I taken today to manage my condition in a healthy way?* or *How have I navigated tough days before?* can help reveal new strategies for coping, even if the issue cannot be fully resolved.

In a complex relationship, such as co-parenting with an ex-partner, asking questions like *What actions did I take, and what actions did my ex-partner take that maintained a respectful interaction focused on our child's needs?* or *How have I managed to communicate calmly in intense situations before?* can help you reflect on what worked. Additionally, *How did I stay composed in those moments?* helps you recognize your own strengths in handling difficult situations.

In more toxic relationships, you may choose to limit or reshape the presence of a person in your life. Reflective questions like *What would setting stronger boundaries look like?* or *What do I need from this relationship to feel supported?* can help you take decisive action to protect your emotional well-being.

Regularly using solution-focused questions allows you to take control of how these presences influence your internal world. By doing so, you transform obstacles into opportunities for growth, reclaim ownership of your narrative, and find clarity in situations that once felt overwhelming.

The Power of Presence Through Micro-Conversations

Though seemingly small and impermanent, brief connections nurture relationships and offer unexpected delights, creating meaningful connections in simple yet powerful ways. Often, it's these everyday exchanges—micro-conversations—that carry more significance than is immediately apparent. Far more than just words, they represent presences woven into the fabric of daily life, with the power to uplift and energize. Each smile, compliment, or kind word serves as a reminder that we are seen, valued, and connected to those around us.

For example:

- At the grocery store, acknowledging the cashier's hard work not only lifts their spirits but also strengthens your sense of community.
- At work, appreciating a colleague's thoughtful collaboration on a challenging project fosters camaraderie and the sense that you're part of something bigger than yourself.
- With neighbors, complimenting their garden brings a shared presence to your street.
- During travel, recognizing a flight attendant's efforts makes the journey feel more humane.
- With family, a simple expression of gratitude toward your spouse provides emotional support, strengthening your bond and reinforcing your partnership.

Though brief, these micro-conversations have a subtle yet lasting influence. Each small exchange quietly strengthens your inner resilience, fostering meaningful connections that ground you. They act as gentle reminders of the power in kindness and shared understanding. By engaging in these fleeting moments, you lift your mood, ease anxieties, and build the confidence to approach others with openness. Over time, these interactions deepen your sense of belonging, empowering you to embrace each connection with renewed positivity.

Enhancing Connections with Micro-Conversations

Building meaningful connections through micro-conversations may seem straightforward, though in practice, it can sometimes feel difficult, especially when balancing the demands of work, family, or unexpected life changes. These brief micro-conversations offer warmth and presence, yet they also require intention and openness—qualities that can be more elusive when your mind is distracted or pulled in many directions. Even these small, thoughtful interactions can serve as a gentle way to nurture bonds with those around you.

This exercise invites you to approach conversations with compassion, both for yourself and others. As you practice these steps, appreciate your own efforts—small actions will gradually lead to more meaningful, empathetic exchanges. Acknowledge the hard work and progress you've made along the way. You may want to jot down your thoughts in a journal as you reflect to keep track of how these small interactions build a stronger sense of community and belonging in your daily life.

Set an intention. Decide to create brief, positive interactions throughout your day, whether with a family member, friend, cashier, or a fellow commuter. Setting this intention helps to foster a mindset of openness and empathy.

Engage with gratitude. Seek opportunities to show appreciation through simple compliments and thoughtful, empathic "for you" statements that highlight the value others bring. A comment like "I noticed how you handled that situation with such grace—it must have been challenging for you. How did you manage it?" acknowledges their effort and invites them to reflect on their strengths. These moments of intentional gratitude, using solution-focused skills, are kindness in action.

Indirect compliments (such as "Where did you learn the skill to work so quickly in the grocery line?" or "How do you maintain your energy throughout the day and still treat customers with such kindness?") emphasize the unique qualities people bring to everyday moments. These reflections deepen connections and foster mutual respect and recognition.

Reflect on your conversations. At the end of the day, take a moment to appreciate the positive micro-conversations and the quiet presences they introduced into your life. Reflecting on these small moments can deepen your awareness of how they foster meaningful connections in your daily interactions. Consider the following guiding questions:

- Were these conversations enriching for you or the other person?
- How did you nurture these moments of connection and the quiet presence they carried?
- How can you continue to invite more of these meaningful presences into your daily interactions?

Visualize a future conversation. Imagine the next interaction you'll have with someone, perhaps a colleague or a family member. Think of a specific compliment or expression of gratitude you could offer. For instance, "I really appreciated how patient you were with that situation. It must have required a lot of effort for you." Taking time to reflect and visualize creates an intention for future conversations, deepening your sense of connection and empathy toward others.

As enriching as brief positive exchanges with strangers or casual acquaintances can be, it's the interactions we have with those closest to us that truly sustain and nourish us. These are the people who make up our inner circle—the ones we turn to for support, advice, and connection. But who are these people, and how do you identify them?

Your Most Important Presences: Introduction to VIP Mapping

VIPs affect your life in powerful ways, both positively and negatively. Imagine these VIPs as the audience at a concert where you're the headliner. Those most influential sit in the front row. Some of these presences are your loudest cheerleaders; others might heckle or throw tomatoes. Though the less central influences are seated further back, like the audience in the balcony, they still play a role in your life.

By recognizing and naming your VIPs, you become more attuned to their influence on your life. This awareness empowers you to harness the support of those who uplift you, manage the challenging presences you cannot avoid, and release those that no longer serve your well-being. In this section, we'll explore how VIPs—both positive and challenging—shape your journey.

VIP mapping is a powerful tool for identifying and organizing the important presences in your life. This process can help you understand how these connections influence your well-being, providing a structured way to reconnect and leverage these relationships for emotional support and improved mental health. By understanding the different types of VIPs, you gain a clearer picture of your social network and can better appreciate the roles each presence plays in your life.

Yourself as a VIP

You're your most important VIP, a truth often overlooked in the demands of daily life. Prioritizing self-care isn't an act of selfishness but one of self-compassion and preservation. By nurturing your mental, emotional, and physical well-being, you build resilience and create the foundation for navigating challenges such as anxiety and stress. Whether through exercise, mindfulness, or meaningful connections with loved ones, caring for yourself enhances your ability to show up fully for others. Recognizing yourself as a VIP honors your individuality and the essential role you play in shaping your own journey. This focus on well-being empowers you to face life's complexities with clarity, purpose, and strength.

Positive Presences: Family, Friends, and Front-Row Support

Very Important Positive Presences (VIPPs) are the trusted individuals and forces that bring support, empathy, and companionship to your life. They include family, friends, mentors, coworkers, and anyone else who shares the front-row seats of your journey. These VIPPs are the ones who lift you up during tough times, celebrate your successes, and listen with compassion when you need it most. They believe in you when you doubt yourself, bring joy in moments of darkness, and offer laughter and courage when you need it most.

VIPPs not only provide emotional support but also offer diverse insights and guidance, often illuminating alternative solutions you may not have considered. They challenge your assumptions, broaden your perspectives, and share specialized knowledge, helping you navigate obstacles more effectively. They serve as anchors, keeping you grounded, focused on your goals, and helping you evaluate your progress.

For example, your best friend who always knows how to brighten your mood, a colleague who offers wise advice, or a mentor who guides you through challenges are all VIPPs. These positive presences empower you to move forward, encourage you to fulfill your dreams, and offer a shoulder to cry on during your darkest days. Through their unwavering support and encouragement, they boost your confidence and help you face life's challenges with strength and resilience.

Spiritual Presences as VIPs

Very Important Spiritual Presences transcend the physical world, holding a profound place in your life. These connections—whether with loved ones who have passed, pets no longer by your side, or even past versions of yourself—continue to shape who you are today. Though they exist beyond time and space, their presence lingers, offering guidance, comfort, and purpose.

Honoring these spiritual VIPs through small rituals or moments of reflection keeps their influence alive. A simple gesture like carrying a photo of a loved one, visiting a meaningful place, or reflecting on your younger self can maintain a sense of connection. These spiritual presences, though transformed, still guide and support you, reminding you of the love and wisdom that transcend physical absence.

Community as a VIP

Community VIPs are the individuals and groups that anchor you in a sense of belonging and support, enriching your life through meaningful connections in your neighborhood, workplace, social circles, and spiritual communities. By identifying and nurturing these presences, you can create stronger bonds that provide emotional support, reduce stress, and bring joy and fulfillment to your everyday life:

- In your neighborhood: Who in your community makes you feel like you belong? It could be the neighbor who always waves hello and stops for a chat, or the family down the street who invites you to their backyard barbecues.
- At work: Who are the colleagues you rely on for support? Perhaps it's the coworker who always listens when you need to vent, the mentor who offers guidance when you're unsure, or the teammate who jumps in to help when you're swamped.
- In social groups: Which friends and clubs play important roles in your life? Maybe it's the book club where you share lively discussions, the sports team where you celebrate victories and support each other through losses, or the close friends who are always there for a coffee and a catch-up.
- In religious or spiritual communities: What religious or spiritual groups provide you with support and connection? Whether it's the church group that prays together, the meditation circle that meets weekly, or the spiritual mentor who offers wisdom and guidance, these communities help you feel connected to something larger than yourself, offering comfort and a sense of purpose.

Pets as a VIP

Your pets aren't just companions; they can be a profound source of joy and comfort, embodying a form of unconditional love that enriches your life. Research underscores the significance of the human-animal bond, revealing that pets can significantly reduce feelings of loneliness and emotional strain (Friedmann and Son 2009; Koukourikos et al. 2019). This powerful connection is felt in the everyday moments you share.

Imagine the delight of playing fetch in the park, where your dog bounds after the ball, tail wagging exuberantly as it races back to you, eyes sparkling with excitement. Each time they drop the ball at your feet, it feels like a small celebration, a reminder of the simple joys that deepen your bond.

On quieter evenings, when the weight of the world feels heavy, there's nothing quite like curling up on the couch with your cat nestled against your side, their rhythmic purring creating a soothing melody that eases your worries away. These shared experiences—be it a leisurely stroll through the neighborhood, where your dog stops to sniff every intriguing scent, or the comforting warmth of your cat as you read—cultivate a deep connection that transcends words.

By cherishing these moments with your beloved companions, you empower yourself to navigate daily stressors more effectively and maintain emotional balance. The joy they bring acts as a buffer against life's challenges, reminding you that love, in its purest form, often comes with four paws and a wagging tail.

Nature as a VIP

Nature is a presence that deeply connects with and supports your well-being. Studies show that spending time in nature significantly lowers cortisol levels, reduces stress, and improves cognitive function (Annerstedt and Währborg 2011; Detweiler et al. 2012; Keniger et al. 2013). Standing barefoot on a warm beach, you feel the sand beneath your feet and the rhythm of the waves calming your breath. The horizon stretching before you offers space for reflection and clarity.

Under a star-filled sky, nature's vastness shifts your perspective, inviting you to contemplate and find peace. The gentle sound of a flowing stream and the sunlight dancing on its surface create a grounding presence. Even watching birds outside your window connects you to life's delicate beauty, gently drawing your attention from everyday concerns. In these moments, nature becomes a VIP, offering comfort, clarity, and renewal.

Powerful Problematic VIP Presences

In life, certain relationships and conditions act as *Powerful Problematic VIPs* (PPVIPs). These might include chronic illnesses, disabilities, and mental health challenges like depression or anxiety. Broader societal forces such as poverty, racism, pollution, politics, and limited access to health care can also weigh heavily on your energy and daily routines. These presences, requiring thoughtful strategies, planning, and actions, demand the same care and attention you would give a personal relationship.

By naming these challenges as PPVIPs, you shift the perspective. Rather than internalizing blame or guilt, you externalize the issues, seeing them for what they are: external forces that are often outside your immediate control. Recognizing a chronic health condition as a PPVIP, for example, allows you to set clear boundaries and develop proactive strategies to manage its effects. This enables you to distribute your energy wisely, ensuring that the condition doesn't dominate your life. Acknowledging systemic racism as a PPVIP rather than a personal failing can change how you move through the world. Instead of internalizing blame, you might find yourself seeking out community support, learning from those who have faced similar struggles, or using your voice to advocate for change.

As you navigate your journey, you may find yourself ensnared in relationships that sap your energy and leave you feeling trapped, or in connections that tug you in conflicting directions, creating uncertainty about your place within them. Some relationships wear you down, erode your confidence, and spark emotional turmoil—like a partner whose subtle critiques make you doubt yourself or a friend who consistently takes more than they offer.

Ambivalent relationships weave an even more intricate tapestry, blending affection with discord: a friend who supports you yet adds stress, or a family member who provides warmth but also resurrects old wounds. By recognizing these relationships as PPVIPs, you empower yourself to evaluate their effects on your life and make choices—whether to establish boundaries, approach them with a new mindset, or, in some instances, release them altogether.

Two core principles of solution-focused thinking are simple yet effective: if something works for you, do more of it; if it doesn't, do something different. Applying this mindset to both the uplifting and challenging influences in your life keeps you empowered, allowing you to make informed choices. Identifying the full range of your very important presences and asking yourself solution-focused questions help guide your inner dialogue toward making thoughtful decisions about these significant relationships and situations.

VIP Mapping with Elizabeth and Carl

After Carl was diagnosed with MS, he and Elizabeth felt their world shrinking. Simple outings became arduous due to Carl's mobility issues, and their days were consumed with medical appointments, insurance struggles, and the stress of mounting medical bills. Carl felt increasingly trapped by his condition, sinking into depression as he mourned the activities he once enjoyed, such as hiking and visiting friends. Simultaneously, Elizabeth felt overwhelmed by the growing list of daily tasks and the pressure of managing everything on her own. The weight of caregiving, anxiety about Carl's health, and the strain on their relationship left them both feeling exhausted and anxious.

Recognizing the need for change, they decided to try VIP mapping, a strategy that helped them categorize and better understand the relationships and conditions (presences) in their lives. Carl's MS emerged as a PPVIP, impacting nearly every aspect of their daily routines. Tasks that had once seemed simple—like emptying the dishwasher, making dinner, or picking things up off the floor—became monumental challenges for Carl. Initially, he blamed himself for these struggles and felt guilty for not being able to contribute more. Elizabeth wrestled with silent resentment toward the increasing burden while grappling with guilt for her frustrations and questioning if there was something she could have done to slow the progression of Carl's condition.

As they navigated the complexities of living with MS, they realized the profound impact of language on their relationship. By naming MS as a *powerful, problematic, persistent, and likely progressive presence* in their lives, they shifted their frustrations away from each other and toward the condition itself. This pivotal recognition alleviated the burden of blame, allowing them to approach their challenges with greater empathy and compassion.

They became more intentional in the language they used with one another, acknowledging their individual struggles while fostering mutual understanding. Carl expressed, "It's exhausting *for me* just to get through my daily routines," while Elizabeth responded with deep empathy, "I can't imagine how tiring it must be *for you* to have every step require so much mental effort just to walk." Carl, in turn, recognized how difficult it was for Elizabeth to feel imprisoned by MS on certain days, and they both admitted, "This has been so *tiring for both of us*." By using inclusive language, they imbued their conversations with shared empathy.

They also made a conscious effort to acknowledge and celebrate small victories. "I appreciate how *we* made a healthy slow cooker meal that nourished both of us," Carl noted. Elizabeth added, "Using the mobility scooter on *our* local bike path was such a great way to enjoy nature *together.*" They reflected on these moments with intentional gratitude, using phrases like "for me," "for you," and "for us" to emphasize their shared experiences and accomplishments.

In addition, they started asking solution-focused questions: "How did *we* figure out the slow cooker meal?" or "How did *we* work together so well to still walk the dogs?" These questions helped them focus on their strengths and collaboration, reinforcing their connection. By naming MS as a *powerful presence* without letting it define their relationship, Carl and Elizabeth found deeper understanding and solidarity in navigating its challenges together.

Ambivalent Presences. To deepen their conversations, Carl and Elizabeth asked each other to rate, on a scale from 1–10 (with 10 being the best and 1 the lowest), how well they were tending to their own needs while managing their loved ones' concern about his condition. They explored what kept their ratings from being lower. Together, they questioned whether their numbers were good enough and identified one action they could each take to enhance their well-being—both individually and collectively.

As Carl assessed his own emotional landscape, he contemplated the challenges of his relationship with his brother, who was particularly anxious about Carl's condition progressing, while prioritizing his own health. He often expressed empathy with statements like "I understand that hearing about my struggles is hard for you too" and also identified ways he could signal Elizabeth that he needed a change in subject or a break from the visit.

VIPPs. Amid the myriad challenges they faced, Carl and Elizabeth found solace in the very important positive presences of their close family and friends. Their children became a wellspring of joy and motivation. Both of their sons, trained as EMTs, offered invaluable support and reassurance during difficult times. Elizabeth's best friend, with her infectious laughter and unwavering support, provided a much-needed emotional outlet. Carl enjoyed going out to breakfast with his close friend. Sharing stories over pancakes and coffee allowed Carl to step away from his responsibilities for a while, fostering a sense of normalcy and camaraderie that was both rejuvenating and essential. Regularly reaching out to these cherished VIPPs allowed Carl and Elizabeth to draw strength and comfort, reminding them of the love that enveloped them.

Spiritual VIPs. Carl and Elizabeth found comfort in their spiritual VIPs, including Carl's late parents, a beloved mentor, and the memory of their prior pets. Carl often asked himself what these important figures would hope for him and what they would appreciate about how he was handling his challenges. For Elizabeth, her faith provided strength, and she reflected on what God's best hopes for them might be and what God would appreciate about their efforts to cope. These reflections offered both Carl and Elizabeth a deeper sense of peace and support, helping them navigate their difficulties with greater resilience.

Community VIPs. Carl and Elizabeth recognized the importance of their community connections. Carl used a low-cost ride service provided by the town for his medical appointments, giving him time to enjoy conversations with others while allowing Elizabeth to focus on her work without the constant worry about Carl's needs. They also joined a local support group for people with MS, where Carl received practical advice and emotional support while Elizabeth connected with other caregivers, finding solidarity and shared experiences. Their neighbors also offered companionship and practical help, such as delivering meals and helping with their pet, reinforcing their sense of belonging and easing the burden on them.

Pet VIPs. Their dog, Al, who had always brought joy, became a lifeline of comfort during difficult times. Al would curl up beside Carl during his most challenging days, offering warmth and companionship. When Elizabeth felt overwhelmed, Al would nuzzle her gently, reminding her to take a break. His wagging tail and eager greetings at the door provided a daily boost of happiness, showing unconditional love through these simple, consistent actions. Al's presence became a steady source of emotional support, helping them navigate their toughest moments.

VIP mapping illuminated Elizabeth and Carl's understanding of the challenges they faced. By cultivating a tapestry of relationships grounded in understanding and empathy, Carl and Elizabeth learned to affirm their experiences with intention, illuminating the path ahead as they navigated their challenges together.

Incorporating empathetic language and solution-focused questions allowed them to deepen their connections with one another. "For me," "for you," and "for us" statements cultivated empathy in both their individual and shared dialogues. These compassionate exchanges not only reinforced their emotional bonds but also prompted reflective questions like "What do we each need?" This practice served as an anchor, helping them navigate their emotional storms with greater clarity.

Scaling Questions to Leverage Your Very Important Presences

Scaling questions have served as a guiding tool throughout this book, helping you measure your progress and identify small, manageable steps forward. Expanding these questions to incorporate the perspectives of your VIPs—the relationships that significantly influence your life—adds depth and possibilities to your solutions.

Imagine asking your VIPs how they perceive your progress and then placing their responses on a scale from 1–10, with 10 being the best and 1 the worst. Their insights—whether from a supportive friend, a challenging relationship, or a persistent condition like depression—provide a well-rounded view of your strengths and challenges. For example:

- How confident would my friend say I am about taking the next step?
- How well would my mentor say I am managing my anxiety?
- How satisfied would my partner be with how I'm taking care of myself lately?

Scaling these perspectives allows you to see your situation from multiple angles, revealing aspects of your life you might have overlooked. In chapter 6, you'll take a closer look at how scaling can empower you to navigate the complexities of your relationships with clarity and intention.

VIP Mapping

In this exercise, you'll explore the powerful presences in your life—those very important individuals, influences, or conditions that shape your experiences. This exercise encourages you to reflect deeply on how these VIPs affect you and how you can actively manage their influence.

As you navigate each section, keep in mind the guiding questions you have been using throughout this book: *What else? How else? Who else? Where else?* and *When else?*

These questions will help enrich your exploration and broaden your understanding of the possibilities available to you. After you read chapter 6, you may wish to return to this section to work your scale for each VIP. You can use the four-step series of questions there or use the online list at http://www.newharbinger.com/54742. The website also includes even more detailed questions to enhance your VIP map and a creative exercise, "Creating Your VIP Mandala."

Yourself as a VIP

Recognize your achievements.

What are you most proud of?

____

What do you most appreciate about yourself?

____

____

Evaluate your self-care efforts.

What does self-care mean to you?

____

____

What have you done recently to care for your needs?

____

____

How have you maintained or improved your well-being physically, mentally, and emotionally?

____

____

____

Identify key self-care practices.

What do you know is most important for taking care of yourself?

____

____

What steps have you taken to prioritize your self-care?

____

____

____

Consider outside perspectives.

Who would notice that you're taking care of yourself?

____

What would they appreciate about your self-care efforts?

____

____

____

What would they see you doing to take care of yourself?

____

____

____

Reflect on the impact of self-care.

How has taking care of your own needs been helpful for you?

____

____

Scale your self-care.

On a scale from 1–10, how well have you been taking care of yourself?

____

VIPPs

Who are the most important people in your life? List all your most positive relationships.

____

____

____

Appreciate your relationships.

What do you most appreciate about them?

____

____

____

____

____

____

What would they say they most appreciate about you?

____

____

____

Acknowledge their support.

What do they know about you that gives them confidence in your success?

____

____

____

Scale your relationships.

On a scale from 1–10, how satisfied are you with the relationship between you and your VIPPs?

____

PPVIPs

Start by giving yourself self-empathy by acknowledging the challenges your powerful problematic VIPs present. It's important to recognize that they can be hard to navigate. Give yourself permission to express your feelings with "for me" statements, such as: "It's exhausting *for me* to manage my health condition every day." "It's overwhelming *for me* to deal with the unpredictability of this relationship." "It's frustrating *for me* when anxiety affects my ability to focus."

____

____

____

Once you've acknowledged the difficulty, explore these powerful problematic VIPs more deeply by considering the following questions:

Are these presences people, conditions, or both? Examples include depression, a chronic illness, or a challenging relationship.

____

____

What do you know about how these problematic presences affect you and those most important to you?

____

____

____

____

What do you know is most important to understand regarding these presences in your life? Reflect on how they influence your daily life, emotions, and overall well-being.

____

____

____

What do you know about letting them go from your life?

____

____

____

____

What do you know are the options for coping with these presences? List thoughts and actions that have made coping more manageable (or tolerable), even if only slightly.

____

____

____

____

____

____

Scale your relationships.

On a scale of 1–10, with 10 being the best and 1 being the opposite, how effectively have you managed these presences?

____

On a scale from 1–10, with 10 being the most ready and 1 the opposite, how ready are you to let go of this presence if this is an option for you?

____

What would be a satisfactory number for you?

____

What factors help prevent your number from being lower?

____

____

____

____

Spiritual VIPs

Who are your most important spiritual VIPs? List all that come to mind.

Appreciate their influence.

What would they say they most appreciate about you?

What would they say they are most proud of in you?

Scale their influence.

On a scale from 1–10, how well have you incorporated their memory and influence into your present moments?

Pets as VIPs

Identify your pet VIPs:

Reflect on the pets and animals in your life, past or present. What do you most appreciate about them?

Appreciate their perspective.

Suppose your pets could talk; what would they say they most appreciate about you?

What would they say you have done to show them love? List all the ways you have shown them love.

Scale your relationship.

On a scale from 1–10, how satisfied are you with the relationship between you and your pets?

Home as a VIP

Identify your home's features:

What does home mean to you? What are the features of your home that you most appreciate?

Appreciate your spaces.

What rooms and spaces in your home do you most enjoy? How have these spaces been helpful for you?

____

____

____

____

Reflect on your efforts.

How did you create these enjoyable spaces for yourself?

____

____

____

What conversational spaces do you most enjoy in your home? How did you foster these spaces?

____

____

____

____

Scale your home's comfort.

On a scale from 1–10, how satisfied are you with your home as a place of comfort and joy?

____

Nature as a VIP

Identify what you enjoy in nature:

What aspects of nature do you most enjoy? Consider walking in nature, appreciating a garden, or observing wildlife.

____

____

Appreciate meaningful moments.

When have you experienced meaningful moments in nature? How were these moments helpful for you?

____

____

____

____

Reflect on your efforts.

How did you create these moments in nature?

____

____

____

Scale your connection to nature.

On a scale from 1–10, how satisfied are you with your relationship with nature?

____

Community as a VIP

Appreciate your community.

What do you most appreciate about your community?

____

____

Whom do you most appreciate in your community, and what do you appreciate about them?

____

____

____

Acknowledge your contributions.

What are you most proud of contributing to your community?

____

____

____

Scale your satisfaction with your community.

On a scale from 1–10, how satisfied are you with your community?

____

Other VIPs

Beyond family, friends, and work relationships, there are many other presences in your life that can significantly impact your well-being. Understanding and mapping these VIPs can offer valuable insights into how various aspects of your life contribute to your mental and emotional health. Consider the following connections:

- Transportation: What forms of transportation bring you most joy—cycling, walking, or driving? How does your daily commute affect your stress levels or overall mood?
- Food: What foods have brought you the most comfort? What does a healthy relationship with food meant to you? When did you last have a meal that made you feel energized and satisfied? How did you create these nourishing meals?
- Substances: How do these substances impact your physical and mental health? Are they helpful for you and if yes, how so? If not, what is your good reason to continue to use them? How helpful would your positive VIPs say substances are for you on a scale from 1–10, where 10 is the most helpful and 1 is the opposite?
- Social media and technology: What have you found most helpful about engaging with social media? What tells you when you have spent an unhealthy amount of time on social media? How do you manage screen time to balance your mental and emotional health?
- Creative endeavors: What creative endeavors provide an outlet for self-expression and stress relief? How do they contribute to your sense of fulfillment?
- Art and music: What has helped you continue to practice these uplifting endeavors? How helpful are art and music for you on a scale from 1–10, where 10 is the best and 1 is the opposite?

As you've learned in this chapter, "taking care of yourself" encompasses attending to and appreciating the myriad complex and rich presences that shape the tapestry of your life. Embracing solution-focused language and empathetic questioning further enhances this process. By using questions that prompt exploration, you can effectively harness the power of your VIPs—those vital influences in your life. This approach not only helps you clarify your circumstances but also allows you to identify actionable steps to move forward.

In the upcoming chapter, you will delve into "best hope mapping" through a solution-focused lens, building on our previous discussions about best hopes as an inner compass. Prepare to engage with thought-provoking questions that ignite your imagination and invite you to envision a life that transcends your current challenges.

CHAPTER 5

Manifesting Your Best Hopes

Your future is a living creation, shaped by each choice and action as you bring your aspirations to life. Manifesting it is more than just visualizing what you want; it's about actively shaping that vision into reality. For instance, manifesting a healthier lifestyle doesn't end with imagining fitness—it involves meal planning, committing to daily movement, and making sustainable choices. Likewise, manifesting deeper relationships requires reaching out, having meaningful conversations, and showing up with empathy.

In this chapter, you'll refine your best hopes into purposeful actions that guide you toward the outcomes that truly matter—those that align with your deepest desires and values. Through thoughtful exercises and reflective questions, you'll develop the ability to harness your strengths, learn from setbacks, and take intentional steps forward. You'll discover how to transform your thoughts and emotions into decisive actions, building steady momentum toward your vision. Whether planning for a day, a week, or years ahead, you'll learn how to manifest your aspirations within any time frame. These tools will help you shape a purposeful and fulfilling path for yourself and those who matter most. (For even more exercises on defining your best hopes, visit the online resources at http://www.newharbinger.com/54742.)

Defining and Pursuing Your Most Important Aspirations

Best hopes are more than ordinary goals; they are your most thoughtfully refined, specific, and actionable aspirations. Solution-focused language enables you to articulate these aspirations through dynamic, purposeful verbs, as you explored in chapter 2. Rather than focusing on what you want to find relief from—such as feelings of depression, anxiety, or stress—consider shifting your attention toward what you'll actively pursue instead.

By engaging with solution-focused questions, you envision how these positive changes will take root in your life and affect those around you. What will you do differently? How will this transformation benefit the people who matter most? Each step forward becomes clearer. The shift in language serves as a catalyst—it ignites the momentum necessary for deliberate, purposeful action.

During periods of depression and anxiety, envisioning a future may feel elusive, as the weight of the present clouds your perspective and makes it difficult to see beyond immediate challenges. Narrowing your focus to small, manageable actions generates momentum, making larger goals feel more attainable. Hope emerges when you recognize your capacity to take action—no matter how small. By planning for even the next five minutes, you give yourself structure, clarity, and a sense of agency.

Whether you set your sights on the next five minutes, hour, or weeks and months ahead, incorporating time frames into your best hopes empowers you to pinpoint actionable steps for both the immediate and longer-term future. By breaking down your aspirations into specific time frames, you effectively respond to urgent needs while nurturing your medium-term intentions and long-term dreams.

Scaffolding Your Best Hopes

This exercise helps you gradually transform your best hopes—including your emotions, thoughts, and VIPs—into intentional steps. How will these influences guide your decisions today? What steps can you take to transform them into opportunities for growth and progress? Each moment offers a chance to shape your emotions, thoughts, and important presences into deliberate, meaningful choices.

As you begin the following exercises in this chapter, remember to reflect on the "else" questions—*What else? How else? Who else? Where else?* and *When else?*—that you have been practicing throughout the book.

Ground yourself in the present. Begin by centering yourself. Close your eyes, take a few deep breaths, and settle into the present moment. Feel the stillness and ask yourself: *What are my best hopes for this moment?* Reflect on what you need right now.

Choosing your time frame. Start by reflecting on your best hopes within various time frames. Consider the following to help you in setting a time frame that resonates with you right now.

Short-term (next ten minutes to an hour). A short-term time frame allows you to respond to your needs quickly, whether by seeking comfort, finding relief, or expressing gratitude:

- What are my best hopes for the next ten minutes to make this moment a bit more tolerable?
- What are my best hopes for the next ten minutes to fully embrace this positive experience with gratitude?

____

____

____

____

Daily or mid-term (today, this week). Emotions that linger but aren't immediately pressing are mid-term. This time frame helps you maintain balance by aligning your activities—such as work, self-care, or connecting with others—over a few days. It's about pacing yourself so that your energy and mental state remain steady throughout the week. For example:

- What are my best hopes for this week so I can say it was satisfying?
- What are my best hopes for dinner with my friends so I can say it was fun?
- What are my best hopes for my medical appointment so I can say it was helpful?

____

____

____

____

____

Long-term (months, years, or life stages). For deeper reflection and long-term goals, think ahead over months or years. This time frame is for growth, planning, or transitioning into new phases of life. It allows you to envision the broader picture and consider how your actions today can shape your future:

- What are my best hopes for this year so I can say it was productive?
- What are my best hopes for my relationship in the next year so I can say it was loving?
- What are my best hopes for the next stage of my life so I can say it was meaningful?

____

____

____

____

____

____

Honor your emotions with compassion. Recognizing your emotions with self-compassion isn't indulgence; it helps you engage with the insights your comfort and discomfort offer. Take a moment to reflect on your emotions and feelings right now. As you do, practice using "for me" statements to continue the language of self-empathy you learned in chapter 3.

____

____

____

____

Feeling instead. The experience of positive emotions is critical for emotional and physical well-being (Bryant et al. 2005; Silton et al. 2020). The more you reach toward what brings you joy, the more likely you are to experience happiness. Engaging in practices that strengthen these positive emotions can significantly enhance your overall well-being (Alexander et al. 2021).

Reflect on what you'd hope to feel instead of depression, anxiety, frustration, or whatever uncomfortable feelings you're experiencing that are difficult for you. Examine the list of positive emotions below and write which ones resonate with you and represent what you hope to feel instead:

Joy	Gratitude	Contentment
Pride	Love	Optimism
Hope	Excitement	Empathy
Serenity	Amusement	Awe
Compassion	Curiosity	

____

____

If you find yourself wanting to not feel depressed, not anxious, not so stressed, ask yourself what you'd hope to *feel instead.*

Thinking instead. When you notice negative self-talk—such as *I can't do this, I'm not worth it,* or *I'm so stupid*—pause to reflect. Consider the following questions:

- What have I said to myself in the past when I approached my thoughts with more kindness and compassion?
- What encouraging words have I thought and spoken to myself when I was more understanding?
- Who would want me to think and speak more kindly to myself, and what would they want me to say instead?

- Supposing I were talking to myself with compassion and kindness, what would I say?

____

____

____

____

____

____

____

____

Taking the time to address these questions can help shift your inner dialogue toward a more positive and supportive mindset.

Doing instead. Positive emotions and thoughts are powerful, but it's the actions they inspire that truly transform your experience. turning positive feelings and thoughts into meaningful actions, you actively shape the future you envision. This process allows you to align your emotions with your goals. Ask yourself:

- What was I doing the last time I felt positive emotions?
- What was I doing when I was thinking more positively about myself?
- How did I create and nurture that moment?
- Who was I with?
- Who noticed?
- What difference did this make for me and those around me?
- Was it helpful for me and, if so, how was it helpful for me?

- Where was I when I experienced these positive moments?

Evaluating your progress with scaling. Now, assess where you are on a scale of 1–10, where 10 represents engaging in actions that nurture your well-being and 1 represents the opposite. To get even more out of this exercise, revisit it after reading chapter 6 and work the scale.

What number am I at now?

What would be a "good enough" number?

What actions keep my number from being lower?

Throughout this exercise, you've skillfully navigated both your thoughts and your feelings—whether comforting or uncomfortable—using them as signals to transform your inner dialogue into intentional, purposeful actions. Each step has acted as scaffolding, strengthening the bridge that connects you to your best hopes. With every thoughtful action, the structure grows stronger, guiding you steadily toward the future you envision.

Your Best Hopes Across Developmental Stages

Life is a journey that keeps changing and growing. From the excitement and curiosity of being a child to the adventures of discovering who you are as a teenager, and then to the freedom of making your own choices as you grow up, each stage brings valuable lessons that can help you reach your best hopes for yourself.

Childhood and Early Development

As you reflect on your early years, consider the role of both wonder and adversity in shaping your identity. You might ask yourself: *What are my best hopes for keeping that childlike curiosity and imagination alive today?* Then, reflect on how past challenges contributed to your resilience and growth, asking: *What are my best hopes for using those lessons to navigate the difficulties I face now?* By weaving together these two threads—nurturing wonder and drawing strength from challenges—you align with a sense of purpose that helps you let go of what no longer serves you and move forward with clarity.

Adolescence

Adolescence is a time of self-discovery, when you began to explore your identity and shape your values and ambitions. During these formative years, you likely encountered both newfound independence and challenges, learning to navigate relationships, responsibilities, and personal growth. Reflecting on that period, you might ask: *What are my best hopes for continuing to grow, learn, and embrace the strengths I cultivated during my teenage years?* Think about how the resilience and values you began to build then can support your ongoing journey of self-discovery today.

Transition to Adulthood (Early Twenties to Thirties)

As you reflect on your early adulthood, consider how you have shaped your independence, established connections, and made decisions that align with your evolving identity. During this time, you've likely explored career paths, deepened relationships, and laid the groundwork for your future. You might now ask: *What are my best hopes for a long-term relationship, advancing in my career, and staying true to my values?* Reflecting on these aspects can help you embrace the growth you've achieved and remain aligned with the purpose and direction that will continue to guide you forward.

Midlife (Late Thirties to Fifties)

In midlife, typically spanning your late thirties to fifties, you may find yourself navigating the complexities of balancing various roles, nurturing relationships, and reigniting your sense of purpose. This stage often prompts a deeper reflection on how your values and priorities have shifted over time. You might consider questions such as:

- What are your best hopes for maintaining healthy and strong relationships?
- How can you stay motivated in your career?
- What new opportunities can you discover or embrace during this time?
- How do you want to show up as a caregiver for your children or parents, if applicable?

Retirement and Aging

As you enter retirement, it's a natural time to reflect on the impact you've made and consider how you wish to continue contributing to the world. This stage invites you to explore ways to stay connected with your purpose, enjoy the freedom of a new chapter, and focus on the legacy you want to leave behind. You might ask: *What are my best hopes for spending these years meaningfully, creating a legacy I'm proud of, and finding joy in this next chapter?* Or *What are my best hopes for aging with vitality, staying engaged with life, and continuing to prioritize my well-being, even as my body changes? What strategies can I use to adapt to my body's needs while staying active and fulfilled?* Embracing these questions can help you focus on achievable goals, allowing you to approach aging as a period of growth and opportunity.

Late Life and End of Life

As you contemplate your best hopes for a fulfilling and peaceful death, think about what would make this moment meaningful for both you and your loved ones. Consider the following:

- What words would you hope to hear spoken at your memorial service?
- What music would evoke the emotions you wish to share?
- Where would you envision this gathering taking place?
- What legacy do you want to leave behind?
- What elements would create a healing experience for those you leave behind, ensuring your presence continues in their lives?

As you progress through life, your best hopes evolve alongside you. With each developmental milestone, from the early stages of self-discovery to the reflective period of later life, your values and hopes deepen, shaping the decisions you make today. How will you act now to manifest the future you envision? This reflection serves as a reminder that each stage of life offers the chance to align your choices with your best hopes, creating a life of meaning, intention, and fulfillment. Through mindful reflection and purposeful action, you can continue to grow and thrive, regardless of where you are on this ever-changing journey.

Handling the "I Don't Know" Dilemma

The "I don't know" dilemma occurs when you ask yourself, *What are my best hopes?* and find yourself unable to articulate a clear answer. This frustration is common. Often, saying "I don't know" indicates that you need more time for introspection. It can also reflect a mindset focused on problems, where negativity clouds your vision, making it difficult to envision your aspirations.

In these moments, consider the influence of your VIPs. Imagine what they might express as their best hopes for you. This perspective can often clarify your own aspirations, especially when feelings of depression or anxiety obscure your vision and make it hard to see beyond current challenges.

Leveraging Your Relationships

Classic VIPs: Consider the most important people in your life. What would their best hopes be for you? What else would they hope for? What would they most appreciate about you fulfilling your best hopes? What do they know about you that you can fulfill your best hopes?

Spiritual VIPs: Reflect on your spiritual VIPs. What would they say their best hopes are for you? What do they know about you that you can fulfill your best hopes?

Community as a VIP: What are your community's best hopes for you and those who live there? What would they say they most appreciate about your contributions to the community? What difference would your contributions make for you and your community?

____

____

____

____

____

____

____

Pet VIPs: Supposing your pets could talk, what would they say are their best hopes for you? What would they see you doing? What difference would it make between you and your pets when you realize your best hopes?

____

____

____

____

____

____

____

Nature as a VIP: Recognize the interconnectedness of all living beings. How might aligning with the rhythms of nature support your journey toward your best hopes? Consider the planet's hopes for your well-being and the impact of your actions on the environment. What have you done to align your aspirations with the greater good of the planet?

____

____

____

____

____

____

____

When Aspirations Feel Out of Your Control

As you reflect on the influence of your VIPs and the insights they provide, it's important to recognize that your hopes can sometimes feel tied to the actions of others. When you find yourself in this position, it can lead to frustration and a sense of helplessness. By shifting your perspective and focusing on your own responses, you can navigate these feelings more effectively and identify actionable steps to move forward.

When your best hopes feel dependent on someone else's actions—like thinking, *If my partner supported me more, I'd feel better* or *If my boss weren't such a jerk, I'd be fine*—it can lead to a sense of lost agency. A helpful way to reclaim your power is by adjusting the grammar of your thoughts. Use the structure:

Suppose [person/relationship] no longer did [the problematic behavior]; what would I be doing differently?

For example, "Suppose my partner weren't so lazy (notice the agreement—there's no need to challenge this part); what would I be doing differently?" This shifts the focus from what others do to what's within your control. You're not dismissing the problem—you're directing your attention to how you can respond or act differently, allowing you to regain agency.

Let's look at Amanda's story to illustrate this.

How Best Hopes Lead to Self-Empowerment

Amanda was thirty weeks pregnant with her first child and worked full-time as a nursing assistant. When she entered her home, she discovered her partner, Gary, passed out from a drinking binge. Gary had relapsed two months ago, and Amanda had given him what she thought was his last ultimatum. Despite loving Gary and appreciating his efforts, this incident felt worse than before.

When Amanda asked herself what her best hopes were, she thought, *If only Gary would stop drinking, our life would be great.* She asked herself what she would be doing differently if Gary no longer drank. She imagined having more energy for self-care, going on walks, having time to cook, managing finances better, and feeling calm at work, knowing she could return to a stable household.

Reflecting on her best hopes helped Amanda recognize that she had to prioritize her well-being and that of her child. She began to plan for her future, one potentially without Gary, with intention. Amanda looked into potential apartments and researched childcare costs. She also started setting aside money to support her transition. This preparation gave her the confidence to express her needs to Gary and outline what she would do if he didn't maintain his sobriety.

Amanda's journey emphasizes the power of language in shaping your perspective. When you find yourself thinking, *If only my partner would change, my life would be great*, it's crucial to recognize the weight of that statement. While there's no denying the validity of your feelings, this mindset can leave you feeling stuck. Instead, consider rephrasing your thoughts with the word "suppose." This grammatical shift not only validates your experience but also redirects your focus toward actionable steps.

Moving Beyond "If Only" Scenarios

In this section, you'll explore solution-focused language techniques to empower you to navigate goals when it feels like "if only they would change, everything would be great."

Rethinking "If Only"

Identify the blame. Reflect on a situation in your life where you find yourself blaming someone else for your challenges. It could be a colleague, a family member, or a partner. Write a statement that encapsulates this blame, for example, "If my partner understood how depressed I was, my self-esteem would improve."

____

____

Reframe the situation. Using the structure provided, reframe your statement by incorporating the elements of "suppose" and "you be doing differently" to shift the focus toward actionable steps and personal agency. For example, "Suppose my partner understood how depressed I am; what would I be doing differently when my self-esteem improves?"

Suppose ____;

what would I be doing differently when __________________________________?

Your Good Reasons

One way to get beyond "if only" thinking is to explore your motivations. While it may not feel like it now, when you choose to take action, there is often something beneficial for you in that moment. However, it's also true that these "good" reasons may not always serve you in the long run.

Reflect on your good reasons. Take a moment to reflect on past actions that, in hindsight, you might now consider unhelpful. Perhaps you engaged in a conflict that wasn't likely to resolve, neglected your self-care, procrastinated on a project, or continued a habit despite knowing its drawbacks. These choices, however, were motivated by reasons that felt valid and beneficial to you at the time. What were the *good reasons* behind your actions? How did these choices serve you in that moment, even if they didn't support your long-term well-being?

Past action: ______________________________

What were my good reasons for doing this?

____

____

Identify helpful alternatives. Recall times when you managed to engage in more helpful behaviors. What did you do instead? How did you accomplish these more helpful actions? Who would notice when you make helpful choices for yourself? What would they observe you doing?

____

____

____

Remember, there are no mistakes, only learning opportunities. With every challenge comes an opportunity for growth. Understanding your good reasons helps you make positive changes with compassion and kindness.

Confident Decision-Making

Pursuing aspirations often involves choosing between outcomes. These trade-offs significantly shape your best hopes by requiring you to prioritize certain goals and consider what sacrifices you're willing to make. For instance, if your best hope is to achieve a balanced life—balancing career success, personal fulfillment, and healthy relationships—you may need to decide between devoting time to work or spending quality moments with loved ones.

Recognizing these trade-offs allows for informed decisions that align with your values. This next exercise helps you explore your decision-making process, reflect on past choices, and build confidence in making decisions aligned with your values and aspirations.

Evaluating Trade-Offs with Hindsight

Reflect on past decisions. Think back on decisions you've made in the past. Consider the decisions that stand out to you. What decisions are you most proud of?

____

____

____

What made those decisions feel like the right choice? How were those decisions helpful for you?

____

____

____

What were the trade-offs in your decision? How did you manage the trade-offs in your decision?

____

____

How did you make the decision? How did you gather information to inform your decision? How did you think through your decision considering both short- and long-term outcomes?

____

____

____

Who was helpful for you in making your decision? How were they helpful?

On a scale from 1–10, how confident are you that you made the right decision, given what you knew? What is a good enough number? What keeps your number from being lower?

Helpful alternatives. What were your learning opportunities in this decision?

Scale your decision-making skills. Now, consider an upcoming decision you're facing. After reading chapter 6, you can return to this exercise and work the scale.

On a scale from 1–10, how ready are you to make a decision?

What number would be good enough?

What actions keep your number from being lower?

Hindsight allows you to evaluate what worked, what didn't, and whether the trade-offs were worth it. Asking yourself questions like the ones above will provide valuable insights into your decision-making process and reinforce your journey toward your best hopes.

Awakening Hope: The Miracle Question

Has imagining change or seeing beyond the present moment ever felt insurmountable? In these moments, the Miracle Question invites you to envision your best life free of the burdens about the path ahead. Answering and scaling the Miracle Question will bridge your aspirations with practical steps, showing that even in the hardest moments, meaningful change can start with simple, intentional actions.

The Miracle Question was born from a profound encounter between Insoo Kim Berg and a client during a therapy session during the 1980s (Berg and de Shazer 1993; de Shazer et al. 2021). When asked what her best hopes were and how the conversations could be helpful for her, the woman, who had HIV and was facing her mortality alongside caring for three young children, responded with a poignant plea: she needed a miracle. Moved by her client's raw honesty, Berg adopted her client's exact words to craft a timeless inquiry that has since become a cornerstone of solution-focused therapy.

The question unfolded something like this:

> *Suppose, tonight, while you are sleeping (so you're totally unaware of it), a miracle happens—the problems that prompted you to talk to me today are resolved. [pause] So, when you wake up tomorrow morning, and as you're going through your day, what will you be doing? What would you notice? Who would notice? What would they notice you doing?*

Surprisingly, the client, initially overwhelmed with distress, began to articulate practical steps she would take. She spoke of seeking support for her children, planning for their needs, and cherishing moments with them.

When people struggle to envision their hopes, the Miracle Question allows them to articulate what they want without burdensome worries, negative self-talk, regrets, and feelings of hopelessness. By integrating scaling questions, you can transform these aspirations into actionable plans.

Envisioning Your Miracle

Before you begin, take a moment to center yourself. Breathe in deeply, allowing your mind to calm, and slowly exhale any lingering tension.

Imagine this: As you complete your evening routine, settle into bed, and gently drift into sleep, a miracle unfolds—one you weren't aware had taken place. When you awaken and find yourself lying in bed, you discover that the problems you've been facing have been resolved.

What is the first thing you notice as you are lying in your bed?

____

____

As you go through your day, what would you be doing that would tell you a miracle has happened?

____

____

____

____

Who would notice this miracle?

____

____

What would your VIPs notice that would tell them a miracle had happened?

____

____

____

____

____

____

What would be different between you and your VIPs after this miracle has happened?

____

____

____

____

____

____

After reading chapter 6, you can revisit this exercise to scale your miracle.

Throughout this chapter, you've embarked on a journey of introspection and self-discovery. As you continue to explore your best hopes, you'll find the beauty and significance of each moment in your life. The online resources for this book (http://www.newharbinger.com/54742) include even more exercises to practice best hope mapping, including a summary of the exercises in this chapter for quick reference, an exercise using scaling to craft your vision, a reflection on what you know and have tried, and creative activities to help you envision your miracle.

In chapter 6, you'll delve into the transformative power of solution-focused scaling, a cornerstone of SFBT. Building on the insights you've already gained, this chapter will further enhance your skills in utilizing scaling questions. As you explore diverse scaling techniques, including coping scales, wellness scales, and satisfaction scales, you'll expand your understanding of their practical applications across various contexts.

CHAPTER 6

Scaling for Success: Creating a Plan One Small Step at a Time

Amid life's complicated challenges, when anxiety and depression weigh heavily and clarity seems hard to find, solution-focused scaling offers a clear path forward. Solution-focused scaling questions redirect your attention from the overwhelming burden of your struggles to the inherent agency within you.

Scaling questions are incredibly valuable tools in your journey, as they're based on your unique perceptions (Berg and de Shazer 1993). When you rate your hopes and goals on a scale, you empower yourself to take control of your own path. This approach ensures that your aspirations align with what matters most to you, boosting your motivation and confidence to make changes. Additionally, solution-focused scaling questions help foster agreement between you and others involved in your endeavors. They also defuse intense emotions by engaging your frontal lobe through numerical discussions and calming your amygdala—remember the upstairs of your brain that you learned about in chapter 3? By utilizing solution-focused scaling questions, you'll likely find that the emotional intensity surrounding difficult conversations lessens significantly.

On the solution-focused scale of 1–10, where 10 signifies mastery and 1 indicates the opposite, the ambiguity surrounding the definition of "1" allows you to focus on your desired outcomes rather than what you wish to avoid. Rather than fixating on the difficulties associated with being at a "1," you actively reflect on your unique strengths and the practical solutions that align with your goals. This approach not only clarifies your direction but also boosts your motivation as you envision the positive changes you seek. Instead of measuring the intensity of challenges like depression, anger, or anxiety, solution-focused scaling questions focus on your ability to stay calm, cope with anxiety, and engage in critical thinking.

In solution-focused conversations, it is important to begin with *assessing your state*, *tapping into your agency and resource activation* (what's worked before), and *leveraging outside perspectives* (VIPs' viewpoints), all of which you've already worked on throughout this book.

It's only *after* you have explored these resources that it is time to plan ahead.

Shifting from Problem Severity to Your Desired Results

You're probably familiar with pain scales used by health care providers to ask how severe your pain is on a scale of 1–10. Evaluating your mental and physical health is essential for effectively managing your well-being—but as you've seen throughout this book, *how* you ask scaling questions can significantly impact your perspective. Solution-focused scales are designed to highlight your best hopes and use your positive language within the question. Unlike problem-focused scales that use the verb "to be," solution-focused scales employ action-oriented verbs. This helps you shift your focus from what's wrong to what you can achieve.

Let's illustrate this with examples related to depression and anxiety.

Problem-focused scaling question: "How severe is your anxiety, from 1–10, where 10 is the highest?"

Solution-focused scaling question: "How well have you been managing your anxiety, from 1–10, where 10 means you can manage very well and 1 is the opposite?"

The problem-focused question centers on the severity of anxiety, which can feel overwhelming and discouraging. However, the solution-focused question uses action-oriented language like *manage*, emphasizing your potential to take practical steps forward.

Problem-focused scaling question: "How tired do you feel, from 1–10?"

Solution-focused scaling question: "How satisfied are you with your energy for your day, on a scale of 1–10, where 10 is very satisfied and 1 is the opposite?"

The problem-focused question measures fatigue levels in this example, which can feel like a dead end. In contrast, the solution-focused question encourages you to think about what's working and how you can build on that satisfaction. (There is a side-by-side comparison of a traditional versus solution-focused health questionnaire at the website, http://www.newharbinger.com/54742.)

By focusing on positive language and action-oriented verbs, solution-focused scaling questions empower you to recognize your strengths and take active steps toward your goals. This approach is not about ignoring problems but about finding ways to move forward despite them.

The table below presents translations of problem-focused scaling questions into solution-focused language, demonstrating how a subtle shift in wording can transform the focus from the severity of a problem to the potential for agency and solutions. Reframing scaling questions to emphasize your agency, strengths, and solutions empowers you to recognize your capacities and take proactive steps toward achieving your goals.

Problem-Focused Scaling	Solution-Focused Scaling
How angry do you feel, from 1–10, where 10 is the angriest you have ever felt?	How *well* do you *calm down*, from 1–10, where 10 means you manage very well and 1 is the opposite?
How suicidal do you feel, from 1–10, where 10 is the most?	How *confident* are you that you can *keep yourself safe*, from 1–10, where 10 is very confident and 1 is the opposite?
How difficult is it for you to take your medications, from 1–10?	How *well* do you *remember* to take your medications, from 1–10, where 10 is always and 1 is never?
How difficult is it to concentrate, from 1–10?	How *well* can you *concentrate and focus* from 1–10, where 10 you are very satisfied and 1 is the opposite?
How poorly are you sleeping, from 1–10?	How *well* have you been *sleeping* from 1–10, where 10 you are satisfied and 1 is the opposite?

Solution-focused scaling questions are designed to be quick, simple, and effective. They help you take charge by identifying effective actions and suggesting small steps to create an action plan. You define what a 3, 7, or 10 means in terms of progress toward your goals. These questions minimize language confusion and can help you access the rational part of your brain more easily, which can help calm your amygdala storms.

The rest of this chapter will take you through a few scenarios to demonstrate the power of scaling, particularly the four-step process of working the scale. And as always, don't forget to intensify your answers with the questions *What else? How else? Who else? Where else?* and *When else?*

You can find a couple more exercises (crafting your vision, scaling to work through decisions privately, creating your courage hierarchy, and scaling your safety) at the website: http://www

.newharbinger.com/54742. To get the most out of this book, you can also revisit exercises in earlier chapters and work your scales.

Using Scaling to Make Decisions

The pressure to make the "right" choice "right now" can heighten anxiety and fear of making mistakes with potentially undesirable consequences. Finding a balance between taking calculated risks and exercising caution is often difficult. By navigating life's numerous choices with thoughtful deliberation and discernment, you can experience heightened confidence in your decision-making.

Enhancing Decision-Making Confidence Through Scaling

Navigating decisions can be complex and lead to decisional anxiety, uncertainty, or stress when faced with making a choice. Decisional anxiety is a common struggle that many people experience. It can manifest in various aspects of life, ranging from significant life decisions to everyday choices. Consider a few of the many decisions people are faced with:

- Where to live
- Career choices
- Employment
- Pet ownership
- Civic engagement
- Seeking help
- Relationships
- Health care decisions
- Daily choices
- Investing time and energy
- Personal health
- Home and garden

Reflect on an upcoming important decision. It may be for today, this week, this month, or in the years to come. You decide the time frame that works best for you. What decision are you thinking about?

____

____

What do you know is most important for you when making this decision?

____

____

What do you know are the most important trade-offs in this decision?

____

____

Reflect on your past decisions that involved trade-offs. What did you learn from those decisions?

____

____

What was most helpful in making those decisions?

____

____

How did you make those decisions?

____

____

What would tell you that you made the right decision?

____

____

What would you be doing that would indicate that you made the right decision?

____

____

Work your decision-making confidence scale.

Assessment

On a scale from 1–10, where 10 is you are confident and ready to make a decision and 1 is the opposite, what number are you at?

____

What is a good enough number for you?

____

What are you doing at that good enough number?

____

____

Activating Your Agency and Resources

What keeps your number from being lower?

____

____

Leveraging Outside Perspectives

Who would notice when you made this decision?

____

What would they see you doing that would tell them this was the right decision for you?

____

____

____

____

Suppose they were asked to rate your decision-making confidence from 1–10, what would they say?

____

What would be different between the two of you, supposing you were at a good enough number?

____

____

What would they say would be a good enough number?

____

Planning Your Next Steps

If your number is not good enough, what is one thing you could do to raise your number by one point?

____

If your number is good enough, what do you want to keep doing?

____

____

On a scale from 1–10, how confident are you that you can take one step to increase your number? What gives you this confidence?

____

____

____

Using Scaling to Help Manage Conflict

Conflict is a natural part of human relationships. Conflicts with people who are important to you—your VIPs—can send you into the basement of your brain and cloud your judgment. Words can fly out impulsively, making it even more difficult for you to express your needs and listen to what others need from you.

Engaging in the scaling process can help calm these emotional storms. By focusing on specific numerical ratings, you step back from the intensity of your emotions and activate the rational part of your brain.

As you reflect on Marilyn's story, consider how you can apply similar strategies to your own life. Engaging in the scaling process can help you clarify your priorities, manage conflicts, and ultimately align your actions with your best hopes.

Marilyn's Dilemma: Navigating Elder Care with Scaling

Marilyn felt overwhelmed by decisions regarding her elderly father's care. His progressive dementia forced her to choose between keeping him at home with additional support or moving him to an assisted living facility. Marilyn struggled to balance the needs of her father, his caregivers, her children, and her work responsibilities. Frequent arguments with her siblings, each with differing opinions on their father's care, compounded her stress.

To facilitate a calm discussion, Marilyn employed solution-focused scaling questions. She first acknowledged each sibling's contributions: her brother managed medical appointments and home maintenance, while her sister took care of finances and visited regularly. Then, she asked them to rate their confidence in several aspects of elder care on a scale from 1–10. Specifically, she inquired about their father's ability to stay at home, the caregivers' effectiveness, and their ability to manage financial costs. They also reflected on their father's, their late mother's, and even the dog's perspectives.

Although their responses varied, they collectively agreed that a rating of 7 felt good enough. They explored what prevented their numbers from being lower and expressed gratitude for the reliable caregivers, medical team, and home modifications. They then identified actionable steps to enhance their father's care: increasing nursing help, installing handrails, purchasing wheelchair ramps, and devising a sustainable financial plan for additional medical expenses.

By scaling perspectives and using VIP mapping, Marilyn and her siblings transformed their anxiety and disputes into practical steps to support their father while being sensitive to each person's needs. This solution-focused approach enabled them to navigate challenging conversations constructively and reach consensus.

This next exercise helps you navigate conflicts with empathy, positivity, and better communication.

Scaling Conflict Resolution

Validate each other's feelings. Reflect on a recent conflict and its emotional impact on you and one of your VIPs. Write down two "for me" statements for yourself and two "for you" statements for your VIP, for example, "It was stressful *for me* to advocate for my needs while feeling discounted," or "It must have been frustrating *for you* to feel like you weren't being appreciated."

____

____

____

____

____

Give compliments. Reflect on what you appreciate about each other. Provide both direct and indirect compliments to each other.

____

____

Work your conflict resolution scale.

Assessment

How well did you manage the conflict on a scale of 1–10?

____

What is a good enough number for you?

____

What are you doing at that good enough number?

____

____

Activating Your Agency and Resources

What keeps your number from being lower?

____

____

Leveraging Outside Perspectives

Who would notice your number?

____

What would they notice you doing at that good enough number?

Suppose they were asked to rate your conflict resolution skills from 1–10, what would they say?

What would be different between the two of you, supposing you were at a good enough number?

What would they say would be a good enough number?

Planning Your Next Steps

If your number is not good enough, what is one thing you could do to raise your number by one point?

If your number is good enough, what do you want to keep doing?

On a scale from 1–10, how confident are you that you can take one step to increase your number? What gives you this confidence?

____

____

____

Carl and Elizabeth: Strengthening Relationships Through Scaling

Think back to Carl and Elizabeth. Elizabeth's chronic anxiety about Carl's declining functionality and his struggle with depression due to his limited mobility were causing significant strain.

After one particularly hard evening filled with arguments and tears, they recognized the need for an honest conversation about their needs. Carl communicated his need for Elizabeth to prioritize self-care, recognizing that her well-being was essential for both of them. Elizabeth expressed her need for Carl to articulate his desires, seek help when necessary, and consider additional support at home.

They incorporated a daily scaling exercise into their routine to ensure they remained on a positive path. Carl rated how well he was articulating his needs each day on a scale from 1–10, while Elizabeth rated her self-care efforts. They would then discuss their ratings and work their scales with each other, providing mutual support and encouragement.

This simple yet powerful practice helped them clarify their expectations, appreciate each moment mindfully, and respond to each other's needs with greater compassion and understanding. By identifying and naming specific actions, they navigated their challenges with more depth and love.

Using Scaling for Improving Relationships

By reflecting on conflicts and relationship satisfaction, you can transform disagreements into opportunities for growth. This process helps you gain insights into navigating conflicts and building stronger, more satisfying relationships.

Evaluating Your Relationship Satisfaction

Name your needed verbs. Reflect on the actions (verbs) you need from your partner and what they need from you. For example: "I need you to empty the dishwasher on nights I come home exhausted from work" and "I need you to ask for help when you feel exhausted." List the verbs you each need from one another.

____

____

____

____

____

____

____

____

____

On a scale of 1–10, how confident are you that you will incorporate each of your verbs with one another?

____

Now, work your relationship satisfaction scale.

Assessment

How well did you manage the conflict on a scale of 1–10?

____

What is a good enough number for you?

____

What are you doing at that good enough number?

____

____

Activating Your Agency and Resources

What keeps your number from being lower?

____

____

Leveraging Outside Perspectives

Who would notice your number?

____

What would they notice you doing at that good enough number?

____

____

____

____

Suppose they were asked to rate your relationship satisfaction from 1–10, what would they say?

____

What would be different between the two of you, supposing you were at a good enough number?

____

____

What would they say would be a good enough number?

____

Planning Your Next Steps

If your number is not good enough, what is one thing you could do to raise your number by one point?

____

If your number is good enough, what do you want to keep doing?

____

____

On a scale from 1–10, how confident are you that you can take one step to increase your number? What gives you this confidence?

____

____

____

Using Scaling for Emotion Regulation

Scaling can help you take small, practical steps to improve your emotional well-being. Remember, every small step counts and contributes to your overall resilience and happiness.

Enhancing Emotional Regulation Skills

Acknowledge the intensity of your emotions. Write down at least two "for me" statements that validate your struggles. For example, "It was terrifying *for me* to learn about my partner's cancer diagnosis."

____

____

Scale your emotional regulation skills.

Assessment

Evaluate how well you navigate life's challenges by rating yourself on a scale of 1–10, with 10 being the best.

____

How well do you manage strong emotions and physical sensations without acting on them immediately?

____

How well can you identify when stepping back and regaining composure is necessary?

____

How well can you categorize your emotions into zones (green for calm, yellow for cautious, red for agitated)?

____

What is a good enough number for you?

____

What are you doing at that good enough number?

____

____

Activating Your Agency and Resources

What keeps your number from being lower?

____

Leveraging Outside Perspectives

Who would notice your number?

____

What would they notice you doing at that good enough number?

____

____

Suppose they were asked to rate your emotion regulation from 1–10; what would they say?

____

What would be different between the two of you, supposing you were at a good enough number?

____

____

What would they say would be a good enough number?

____

Planning Your Next Steps

If your number is not good enough, what is one thing you could do to raise your number by one point?

____

If your number is good enough, what do you want to keep doing?

____

On a scale from 1–10, how confident are you that you can take one step to increase your number? What gives you this confidence?

____

____

____

Evaluate your coping skills. Identify your coping skills and rate how well you utilize them during emotionally intense situations:

What actions (verbs) help you manage uncomfortable feelings?

____

____

____

How well have you used these coping skills (from 1–10)?

____

Work your scales.

Embracing your needs through scaling. On a scale from 1–10, how well do you:

Say okay and maintain calm.	______________
Name your emotions with acceptance and compassion.	______________
Identify and recognize your needs and boundaries.	______________
Express your needs assertively and effectively.	______________
Accept and welcome help from others.	______________
Learn from setbacks and pivot your approach.	______________

Rate your mood satisfaction on a scale from 1–10:

How satisfied are you with your mood?	______________
How confident are you that things will work out?	______________
How much do you enjoy fun activities?	______________
How often do you appreciate yourself?	______________
How well do you voice your needs, wants, and opinions?	______________
How satisfied are you with your relationships?	______________

There are countless ways to use solution-focused scaling to build your agency and take practical steps toward making a plan. Whether you're addressing wellness, trauma, substance use, or recovery, scaling can effectively promote self-care. You can visit the website for this book (http://www.newharbinger.com/54742) for a printout of questions to work your scale and for bonus scaling exercises.

In the upcoming chapter, you will learn how to sustain your solution-focused skills and cultivate habits that empower your journey. You'll explore exercises that integrate the questions you've learned and apply them in various contexts, helping you solidify your solution-focused skills.

CHAPTER 7

Building and Sustaining Your Path to Success

Congratulations! You have reached a graduation milestone in your path to equip yourself with solution-focused skills for managing stress, anxiety, and depression. Throughout this book, you've delved into solution-focused tools that give you in-the-moment techniques to help you stay grounded and focus on small, achievable goals to nurture hope.

Let's pause for a moment to contemplate the invaluable skills you've gained thus far. You have mastered the solution-focused language and the art of amygdala whispering. You have recognized and rediscovered your strengths, mapped your VIPs, and appreciated the power of relationships in your life. You have charted your best hopes and learned the power of solution-focused scaling. Your unique solution-focused toolkit empowers you with simple and effective ways to manage intense emotions. It helps you surmount stress, anxiety, and depression and equips you with the skills to flourish despite the obstacles you face.

In this chapter, you'll focus on sustaining your solution-focused skills while cultivating empowering habits that enhance your journey. You'll discover ways to find calm through scaling techniques and draw strength from past, present, and future experiences. Additionally, the chapter will introduce you to the solution-focused four-square approach and the practice of solution-focused debriefing, allowing you to celebrate your growth and progress.

Drawing Strength from the Past, Present, and Future

Solution-focused conversations are a tapestry weaving together the threads of the past, present, and future, each strand infused with intention and mindfulness. Remember those verbs from chapter 2? In moments when you may be withdrawing, struggling to find motivation, ruminating on past regrets, worrying about future events, or overthinking decisions, ask yourself how you *have managed*, even if it was just for the last ten minutes.

Equally important are the present and future, filled with moments worth cherishing. Embrace simplicity by asking, *Who are the most important people and relationships in my life, and what do I most appreciate about them?* Reflect on all your VIP categories to bring a wealth of connections into your present moment. Consider, *What's happening now that I want to continue?* and *What are my best hopes moving forward?* These questions help you mindfully pay attention to your verb tenses, allowing you to chart a path that brings meaning and joy to your life.

Embracing the Now

This exercise invites you to embark on a journey through time—past, present, and future—to unveil the profound reservoir of your inner strength. Within these temporal dimensions, you will discover tales of past resilience, savor the richness of present joys, and paint vivid pictures of your future aspirations. By crafting these tenses with intention, you will unlock the beauty of your inner strength, allowing you to gracefully navigate the ever-changing landscapes of life's challenges.

Embracing your past tense.

When did you last experience joy, even for a short time?

____

When did you notice things were even a little bit more bearable?

____

____

How did you bear it?

____

____

____

Embracing your present tense.

What is happening that you want to continue to happen?

____

____

____

____

Who are the most important relationships in your life?

____

____

How are you nurturing and sustaining these present positive elements?

____

____

____

____

Embracing your future tense.

What are your best hopes for the next day, week, month, or even the next ten minutes?

____

____

____

____

What actions would you take to bring your best hopes to life?

____

____

____

____

As you complete this exercise, take a moment to recognize the power of verb tenses in shaping your life's narrative. By intentionally using these tenses, you can stay grounded in the moment while planning for the future and reflecting on the past.

The Four-Square Solution-Focused Framework

This exercise is designed to combine all the skills you've learned so far in four simple squares. Let me break it down for you. Throughout your journey, you've discovered that solution-focused skills involve three fundamental shifts: an order shift, a paradigm shift, and a language shift.

The order shift means promptly activating your resources with intention and acknowledging and valuing your strengths and the actions that you have already taken to manage the challenges you have faced. These often-overlooked golden-nugget moments are hidden treasures waiting to be recognized, appreciated, and harnessed. Next, the paradigm shift assumes positive outcomes unless proven otherwise—a mindset of optimism and possibility. And then there's the language shift, framing questions and statements in a way that implicitly assumes positive ideas or conditions.

With the four-square solution-focused framework, you'll combine the solution-focused skills you have learned throughout this book. It's a simple and quick method to help you navigate stressful moments when you need immediate tools (see http://www.newharbinger.com/54742 for a template). In this exercise, you'll explore four key steps to unlock your strengths, nurture meaningful connections, envision a brighter future, and take practical steps to make it a reality, one step at a time.

Square 1: Agency and resource activation. Start by folding a piece of paper into four sections, labeling them 1, 2, 3, and 4. Reflect on the past week and write your answers in square 1.

- What did you most enjoy this past week?
- What's happening that you want to continue to happen?
- What's been better this past week?
- What's been even a little bit more bearable this week?
- How have you coped with the challenges you faced this past week?

Square 2: VIP mapping. Next, consider your VIP categories (yourself, positive, spiritual, powerful and problematic, pets, community, and other VIPs) and answer the following questions in square 2:

- Who would notice you enjoying your week, that things are better or more bearable for you, and appreciate how you have been coping with the challenges you faced?
- What do you most appreciate about them?
- What do they know about you that you can succeed and overcome the obstacles you face?
- What would they say they most appreciate about you?
- Supposing we asked them what their best hopes would be for you, what would they say?

Square 3: Best hopes mapping. Envision your best hopes:

- What are your best hopes for today, this week, this month, this year, and the next ten minutes?
- What would you be doing when your best hopes are fulfilled?
- What do you know about yourself that will help you fulfill your best hopes?
- Who would appreciate that you are fulfilling your best hopes?
- What would their best hopes be for you? What do they know about you that you can fulfill your best hopes?

Square 4: Scaling.

Assessment

- Suppose 10 is "you are achieving your best hopes" and 1 is the opposite; where are you now?
- What is a good enough number for you?
- What are you doing at that good enough number?

Activating Your Agency and Resources

- What keeps your number from being lower?

Leveraging Outside Perspectives

- Who would notice your number?
- What would they notice you doing at that good enough number?
- Suppose they were asked to rate your ________ from 1–10, what would they say?
- What would they say would be a good enough number?

Planning Your Next Steps

- If your number is not good enough, what is one thing you could do to raise your number by one point?
- If your number is good enough, what do you want to keep doing?
- On a scale from 1–10, how confident are you that you can take one step to increase your number? What gives you this confidence?

As you conclude this exercise, take a moment to acknowledge the insights you've gained and the progress you've made. Know that you have the strength and resources within you to overcome obstacles and create a fulfilling life. As you progress, carry the lessons from this exercise and continue cultivating hope, agency, and positive change in your journey.

Solution-Focused Debriefing

Solution-focused debriefing means taking a reflective pause after an event or task to discuss what happened, what went well, how you coped with the challenges you faced, what you want to continue to happen, and to share observations and successes.

You can use the solution-focused four-square framework to simplify debriefing. Doing this exercise with a loved one strengthens relationships and aligns with deeper needs and aspirations.

Finding Joy in the Journey: Carl and Elizabeth's Daily Ritual

Carl and Elizabeth found joy and connection in their nightly solution-focused debriefs. Each evening, they reflected on the day using thoughtful questions that highlighted their achievements.

During one such debrief, Elizabeth asked what was better today—a trip to the pool stood out. Carl, usually reluctant to accept help, surprised himself by welcoming the lifeguard's assistance. Even better, the lifeguard offered lessons to others with similar challenges, making their swim sessions a win-win. Carl moved confidently in the water while Elizabeth savored her laps, free from constant worry.

As they engaged in scaling questions about their daily challenges, they discovered how small adjustments, such as embracing support and taking mental breaks, led to significant relief. They asked each other, "How well did we pivot with today's MS challenges, from 1–10?" Working their scales, they discovered that more swims, self-care, accepting help, and intentionally taking mental and physical breaks from the constant worry brought significant relief. They celebrated Carl's newfound ease and Elizabeth's ability to relax.

Daily Debrief

This daily solution-focused debriefing exercise uses a four-square framework to guide reflection, validate actions, and plan for a better tomorrow. Each square focuses on different aspects of the day, incorporating the solution-focused tools covered in the book. Reflect on your day and consider asking yourself the following questions.

Square 1: Activating agency.

General Questions

- What was better today?
- What is happening that should continue?
- How did you cope with the challenges you faced?
- What were today's learning opportunities?
- What were the cherished moments of your day?

Amygdala Whispering
Use "for me" and "for you" statements to validate emotions:

- "That was pretty stressful for me."
- "That seemed like a relief for you."

Compliments

- What direct compliments can you give yourself for what you did well today?
- What indirect compliments can you give yourself? (For example, "How did you manage to stay calm in that situation?")

Positive Differences

- What positive differences did you notice in yourself today?
- How can you build on these positive differences tomorrow?

Square 2: Mapping VIPs.

- Who noticed the positive changes today?
- What do you appreciate about them?
- What did they appreciate about those moments?
- How can you nurture these connections further?

Square 3: Envisioning best hopes.

- What are your best hopes for tomorrow, this week, or even the next ten minutes?
- What do you know about yourself and the situation that your hopes can be realized?
- Consider your VIPs—what would their best hopes be for you? What do they know about you that you can achieve your best hopes?

Square 4: Solution-focused scaling.

On a scale of 1–10:

- How satisfied are you with your day?
- How well did you pivot through today's challenges?
- How confident are you that you will do your best to continue to do those things that bring you joy and work in your life?
- Work your scale by acknowledging your successes and planning how to build on them.

Regularly using this four-square framework will enhance your sense of agency, deepen your relationships, and keep you focused on what truly matters.

Graduation Reflection: Celebrating Your Growth

Congratulations on reaching this significant milestone in your journey! You've made remarkable progress in embracing solution-focused language and supporting yourself with kindness and compassion, and you've gained invaluable skills that will guide you further. Just like learning a language, mastering solution-focused thinking is an ongoing journey of growth and self-discovery (for practice games, visit the website, http://www.newharbinger.com/54742). It's about practicing self-compassion, recognizing your inherent strength, and knowing that you have the power to hold hope in your life.

As you prepare to graduate from this workbook, take a moment to reflect on your confidence in using these skills. Think about where you stand now. On a scale from 1–10, how confident are you that you're ready to move forward? What has been most helpful to you in embracing these skills?

____

____

____

Consider what would make that number feel "good enough" for you. What keeps it from being lower? What would you be doing differently if your confidence increased by just one point?

____

____

____

Now, think about how confident you are (on a scale of 1–10) that you'll continue nurturing these solution-focused skills daily. What gives you this confidence?

____

____

____

Who in your life would notice your ongoing efforts to nurture these skills? What would they most appreciate about your practice of self-compassion and kindness? Finally, what difference would this make for you and those who matter most in your life?

____

____

____

____

____

____

My best hope is that you will continue to appreciate the strength within yourself, the connections you embrace, the agency you hold, and the determination to take one step at a time toward what you need and hope for each day. You hold the potential to tap into your boundless inner strength, overcoming challenges with courage and embracing goals that enrich your life to the fullest. I hope this book has served as a comforting companion in your quest for a more fulfilling life, offering guidance as you navigate the intensity and complexities of anxiety and depression. It's been an honor and a privilege to accompany you on this journey. Thank you for your willingness to learn and embrace the incredible strengths within yourself and those most important in your life.

References

Alexander, R., O. R. Aragón, J. Bookwala, N. Cherbuin, J. M. Gatt, I. J. Kahrilas, N. Kästner, et al. 2021. "The Neuroscience of Positive Emotions and Affect: Implications for Cultivating Happiness and Wellbeing." *Neuroscience & Biobehavioral Reviews* 121: 220–49.

Anderson, H., and H. Goolishian. 1992. "The Client Is the Expert: A Not-Knowing Approach to Therapy." In *Therapy as Social Construction*, edited by S. McNamee and K. J. Gergen, 25–39. New York: Sage Publications.

Annerstedt, M., and P. Währborg. 2011. "Nature-Assisted Therapy: Systematic Review of Controlled and Observational Studies." *Scandinavian Journal of Public Health* 39(4): 371–88.

Berg, I. K., and S. de Shazer. 1993. "Making Numbers Talk: Language in Therapy." In *The New Language of Change: Constructive Collaboration in Psychotherapy*, edited by S. Friedman, 5–24. New York: Guilford Press.

Bryant, F. B., C. M. Smart, and S. P. King. 2005. "Using the past to enhance the present: boosting happiness through positive reminiscence." *Journal of Happiness Studies* 6: 227–260.

Cacioppo, J. T., and S. Cacioppo. 2018. "The Growing Problem of Loneliness." *The Lancet* 391(10119): 426.

Cacioppo, S., A. J. Grippo, S. London, L. Goossens, and J. T. Cacioppo. 2015. "Loneliness: Clinical Import and Interventions." *Perspectives on Psychological Science* 10(2): 238–49.

de Shazer, S. 1988. *Clues: Investigating Solutions in Brief Therapy*. New York: W. W. Norton.

de Shazer, S. Y. Dolan, H. Korman, T. Trepper, E. McCollum, and I. K. Berg. 2021. *More Than Miracles: The State of the Art of Solution-Focused Brief Therapy*. Routledge.

Detweiler, M. B., T. Sharma, J. G. Detweiler, P. F. Murphy, S. Lane, J. Carman, A. S. Chudhary, M. H. Halling, and K. Y. Kim. 2012. "What Is the Evidence to Support the Use of Therapeutic Gardens for the Elderly?" *Psychiatry Investigation* 9(2): 100–10.

Elias, S. M. S., C. Neville, and T. Scott. 2015. "The effectiveness of group reminiscence therapy for loneliness, anxiety and depression in older adults in long-term care: a systematic review." *Geriatric Nursing* 36(5): 372–380.

Feynman, R. P., R. B. Leighton, and M. Sands. 1963. *The Feynman Lectures on Physics*, vol. 1. New York: Addison-Wesley.

Franklin, C., ed. 2012. *Solution-Focused Brief Therapy: A Handbook of Evidence-Based Practice*. Oxford: Oxford University Press.

Friedmann, E., and H. Son. 2009. "The Human–Companion Animal Bond: How Humans Benefit." *Veterinary Clinics of North America: Small Animal Practice* 39(2): 293–326.

Kemeny, M. E. 2009. "Psychobiological Responses to Social Threat: Evolution of a Psychological Model in Psychoneuroimmunology." *Brain, Behavior, and Immunity* 23(1): 1–9.

Keniger, L. E., K. J. Gaston, K. N. Irvine, and R. A. Fuller. 2013. "What Are the Benefits of Interacting with Nature?" *International Journal of Environmental Research and Public Health* 10(3): 913–35.

Kim, J., S. S. Jordan, C. Franklin, and A. Froerer. 2019. "Is Solution-Focused Brief Therapy Evidence-Based? An Update 10 Years Later." *Families in Society: The Journal of Contemporary Social Services* 100(2): 127–38.

Koukourikos, K., A. Georgopoulou, L. Kourkouta, and A. Tsaloglidou. 2019. "Benefits of Animal-Assisted Therapy in Mental Health." *International Journal of Caring Sciences* 12(3): 1898–1905.

Lieberman, M. D., N. I. Eisenberger, M. J. Crockett, S. M. Tom, J. H. Pfeifer, and B.M. Way. 2007. "Putting Feelings Into Words." *Psychological Science* 18(5): 421–428.

Long, L. J., and M. W. Gallagher. 2018. "Hope and Posttraumatic Stress Disorder." In *Oxford Handbook of Hope*, edited by M. W. Gallagher and S. J. Lopez, 233–242. Oxford: Oxford University Press.

Lutz, A. B. 2013. *Learning Solution-Focused Therapy: An Illustrated Guide*. Washington, DC: American Psychiatric Pub.

Park, C., A. Majeed, H. Gill, J. Tamura, R. C. Ho, R. B. Mansur, F. Nasri, et al. 2020. "The Effect of Loneliness on Distinct Health Outcomes: A Comprehensive Review and Meta-Analysis." *Psychiatry Research* 294: 113514.

Powell, W. J. 1872. *Tachyhippodamia: Or, The New Secret of Taming Horses*. Philadelphia: W. R. Charter.

Snyder, C.R., L. M. Irving, and J. R. Anderson. 1991. "Hope and Health." *Handbook of Social and Clinical Psychology: The Health Perspective* 162(1): 285–305.

Stilton, R., I. J. Kahrilas, H. V. Skymba, J. Smith, F. B. Bryant, and W. Heller 2020. "Regulating Positive Emotions: Implications for Promoting Well-Being in Individuals with Depression." *Emotion* 20(1): 93.

Vermeulen-Oskam, E., C. Franklin, L. P. M. van't Hof, G. J. J. M. Stams, E. S. van Vugt, M. Assink, E. J. Veltman, A. S. Froerer, J. P. C. Staaks, and A. Zhang. 2024. "The Current Evidence of Solution-Focused Brief Therapy: A Meta-Analysis of Psychosocial Outcomes and Moderating Factors." *Clinical Psychology Review* 114: 102512.

Weinstein, N., H. Hansen, and T.-V. Nguyen. 2023. "Definitions of Solitude in Everyday Life." *Personality and Social Psychology Bulletin* 49(12): 1663–78.

Zak, A. M., and K. Pękala. 2024. "Effectiveness of Solution-Focused Brief Therapy: An Umbrella Review of Systematic Reviews and Meta-Analyses." *Psychotherapy Research* 1–13.

Anne Bodmer Lutz, MD, is executive director of the Institute for Solution-Focused Therapy, a board-certified child and adolescent psychiatrist, and assistant professor of psychiatry at the University of Massachusetts. Mentored by solution-focused brief therapy founders Insoo Kim Berg and Steve de Shazer, she has spent more than three decades applying this approach across mental health, education, and beyond. Author of *Learning Solution-Focused Therapy*, Lutz trains professionals worldwide, helping them create meaningful change—one conversation at a time.

Foreword writer **Cynthia Franklin, PhD, LCSW-S, LMFT**, is director of external relations and Stiernberg/Spencer Family Professor in mental health in the Steve Hicks School of Social Work at the University of Texas at Austin, courtesy professor in the department of psychiatry and behavioral sciences at Dell Medical School at the University of Texas at Austin, and editor in chief of *Social Work*.

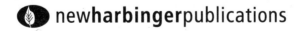

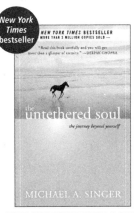

Did you know there are **free tools** you can download for this book?

Free tools are things like **worksheets**, **guided meditation exercises**, and **more** that will help you get the most out of your book.

You can download free tools for this book—whether you bought or borrowed it, in any format, from any source—from the New Harbinger website. All you need is a NewHarbinger.com account. Just use the URL provided in this book to view the free tools that are available for it. Then, click on the "download" button for the free tool you want, and follow the prompts that appear to log in to your NewHarbinger.com account and download the material.

You can also save the free tools for this book to your **Free Tools Library** so you can access them again anytime, just by logging in to your account! Just look for this button on the book's free tools page.

+ Save this to my free tools library

If you need help accessing or downloading free tools, visit newharbinger.com/faq or contact us at customerservice@newharbinger.com.